Peer Reviews of Competition Law and Policy: Dominican Republic

Please cite this publication as:
OECD/IDB (2024), *Peer Reviews of Competition Law and Policy: Dominican Republic*, OECD Publishing, Paris, https://doi.org/10.1787/18f04007-en.

ISBN 978-92-64-61292-1 (print)
ISBN 978-92-64-76760-7 (pdf)
ISBN 978-92-64-97453-1 (HTML)
ISBN 978-92-64-78078-1 (epub)

Corrigenda to OECD publications may be found on line at: www.oecd.org/about/publishing/corrigenda.htm.

Foreword

The OECD has been active in promoting competition policy in countries across Latin America and the Caribbean (LAC). The partnership between the OECD and the Inter-American Development Bank (IDB) has advanced these efforts. In competition matters, the annual Latin American and Caribbean Competition Forum (LACCF) has been a cornerstone of this collaboration. This unique forum brings together senior officials from countries in the region, to promote and support the identification and dissemination of best practices in competition law and policy. Twenty-one meetings have been held to date.

The OECD and the IDB have collaborated on a series of reviews of competition law and policy regimes in LAC since 2003. Peer Reviews are founded upon the willingness of a country to submit its laws and policies to substantive review by other members of the competition international community. This process provides valuable insights to the country under study and promotes transparency and mutual understanding for the benefit of all. There is an emerging international consensus on best practices in competition-law enforcement and the importance of pro-competitive reform. Peer Reviews are an essential part of this process, as well as an important tool in strengthening competition institutions. Strong and effective competition institutions can promote and protect competition throughout the economy, which increases productivity and overall economic performance. This is consistent with the policies and goals of the OECD and the IDB to support pro-competitive policy and regulatory reforms, which will promote economic growth LAC markets.

Peer Reviews are a regular part of the LACCF. In 2007, the LACCF assessed the impact of the first four Peer Reviews conducted at the LACCF on Brazil, Chile, Peru and Argentina, and the Peer Review of Mexico, which was conducted at the OECD's Competition Committee. The Forum then reviewed El Salvador in 2008, Colombia in 2009, Panama in 2010 and Honduras in 2011. A follow-up of the nine Peer Reviews was conducted in 2012 as part of the LAACF's 10th anniversary. In 2014, 2018 and 2019, Costa Rica, Peru and El Salvador had their competition regimes peer reviewed, respectively. In 2020, Ecuador was the latest country to be peer reviewed at the LACCF before the Dominican Republic.

This report served as basis for the Peer Review in the presence of lead examiners that took place at the 21st Latin American and Caribbean Competition Forum on 28 September 2023 in Quito, Ecuador. The lead examiners were Jorge Grunberg Pilowsky (National Economic Prosecutor, FNE, Chile), Guillermo Rojas Guzmán (Commissioner, COPROCOM, Costa Rica) and Andrea Marván Saltiel (Chair Commissioner, COFECE, México). The delegation representing the Dominican Republic during the Peer Review session was led by: Maria Elena Vásquez Taveras (Chairwoman, Pro-Competencia), Fior D'aliza Alduey (Executive Director, Pro-Competencia), José Beltré (Director of Competition Advocacy, Pro-Competencia) and Pedro Luis Montilla Castillo (Senior Legal Advisor, Executive Branch).

The OECD and the IDB would like to thank the lead examiners and all other officials that participated in the Peer Review examination. The OECD and the IDB are also grateful to the Dominican Republic's Pro-Competencia for their valuable input, availability to answer queries, and support in facilitating interviews. Finally, the OECD and the IDB would like to thank all the stakeholders who accepted to participate in the meetings that took place during the fact-finding mission, held in the Dominican Republic from 27 to 31 March 2023, and who contributed to the completeness and the accuracy of the report.

The report was prepared by Iratxe Gurpegui (IDB Consultant) with research support by Vivian Ianelli, and reviewed by Marcelo Guimarães and Paulo Burnier, under the strategic supervision of Ori Schwartz (all from the OECD Competition Division). Mario Umaña (IDB) also provided valuable inputs throughout the entire Peer Review process.

Table of contents

FIGURES

TABLES

BOXES

Abbreviations and acronyms

ACODECO	Authority for the Protection of Consumers and Defence of Competition (*Autoridad de Protección al Consumidor y Defensa de la Competencia*), Panama
AIRD	Association of Industries of the Dominican Republic (*Asociación de Industrias de la Republica Dominicana*)
AIPARC	Association of Water Purification Industry of the Cibao Region (*Asociación de la Industria de Purificación de Agua en la Región de Cibao*)
APORDOM	Dominican Port Authority (*Autoridad Portuaria Dominicana*)
CADE	Administrative Council for Economic Defence (*Conselho Administrativo de Defesa Econômica*), Brazil
CAFTA-DR	Dominican Republic-Central America Free-United States Free Trade Agreement
CDPC	Commission for Defence and Promotion of Competition (*Comisión para la Defensa y Protección del Consumidor, Honduras*), Honduras
CND	*Cervecería Nacional Dominicana*
CNDC	National Commission for the Competition Defence (*Comisión Nacional de Defensa de la Competencia*), Argentina
CNE	National Energy Commission (*Comisión Nacional de Energía*)
CNMC	National Commission of Markets and Competition (*Comisión Nacional de los Mercados y la Competencia*), Spain
COPROCOM	Commission for Promotion of Competition (*Comisión para Promover la Competencia*), Costa Rica
COFECE	Federal Economic Competition Commission (*Comisión Federal de Competencia Económica*), Mexico
DIGEPRES	General Direction for Budget (*Dirección General de Presupuesto*)
DGA	General Directorate of Customs (*Dirección General de Aduanas*)
DGCP	General Directorate of Public Procurement (*Dirección General de Compras Públicas*)
ENJ	National School for the Judiciary (*Escuela Nacional de la Judicatura*)
IDAC	National Institute of Civil Aviation (*Instituto Nacional de Aviación Civil*)
INDOTEL	Dominican Institute of Telecommunications (*Instituto Dominicano de las Telecomunicaciones*)
INTRANT	National Institute of Inland Transport (*Instituto Nacional de Tránsito y Transporte Terrestre*)
JAC	Civil Aviation Board (*Junta de Aviación Civil*)
LGE	General Electricity Law (*Ley General de Electricidad*)
LMF	Monetary and Financial Law (*Ley Monetaria y Financiera*)
LPI	Industrial Property Law (*Ley de Propiedad Industrial*)
ONAPI	National Office of Industrial Property (*Oficina Nacional de la Propiedad Industrial*)
ONDA	National Copyright Office (*Oficina Nacional de Derechos de Autor*)
PEI	Institutional Strategic Plan (*Planificación Estratégica Institucional*)
PRM	Modern Revolutionary Party (*Partido Revolucionario Moderno*)
Pro-Consumidor	National Institute for the Protection of Consumer Rights (*Instituto Nacional de Protección de los Derechos del Consumidor*)
Pro-Competencia	National Commission for the Defence of Competition (*Comisión Nacional de Defensa de la Competencia*)
SE	Superintendency of Electricity (*Superintendencia de Electricidad*)
SIMV	Superintendency of the Stock Market (*Superintendencia de Mercado de Valores*)
SIPEN	Superintendence of Pensions (*Superintendencia de Pensiones*)
TC	Constitutional Court (*Tribunal Constitucional*)
TSA	Superior Administrative Court (*Tribunal Superior Administrativo*)

Executive summary

This report results from the Peer Review of the Dominican Republic's competition law and policy. It presents the main findings of the current panorama of competition law and policy in the Dominican Republic and concludes with recommendations developed by the lead examiners and discussed at the Peer Review examination, carried out during the 2023 OECD-IDB Latin American and Caribbean Competition Forum.

After 12 years of legislative process, the Dominican Republic adopted its Competition Act in 2008, although it only became fully operational in 2017. Despite the efforts of Pro-Competencia, the Dominican competition authority, competition enforcement is still incipient in the country. While Pro-Competencia has only sanctioned two competition cases, sector regulators with competition enforcement powers have only adopted one enforcement decision related to competition law. No bid-rigging cases have been sanctioned.

There is a lack of overall competition culture in the Dominican Republic. Institutions empowered to enforce competition law (in particular, Pro-Competencia) face significant budgetary and human resources restraints. The Dominican Competition Act also has several limitations. For instance, there is no merger control regime applied to the entire economy, the maximum fines for anti-competitive practices are low and with low deterrent effects, and investigations are subject to a very short statute of limitation and expiration deadline. Furthermore, the competition law framework includes a general competition law regime (enforced by Pro-Competencia) and sector-specific competition law regimes (enforced by key sector regulators). There are still insufficient levels of co-operation between Pro-Competencia and sector regulators in the application of competition law, in addition to concerns on possible conflicting interests and lack of competition expertise within certain regulatory entities with the powers to enforce competition law.

The recommendations relate to the institutional and legal framework, competition law enforcement, as well as competition advocacy and institutional co-operation. They suggest possible ways forward for consideration by the Dominican Republic, with the aim of improving the country's competition law and policy.

Key recommendations

Institutional and legal framework

- Adopt a common competition framework, including both substantive and procedural rules, that uniformly applies across all sectors. In addition, clarify which entities are responsible for the enforcement of competition law in the different sectors (i.e., Pro-Competencia or sector regulators).
- Strengthen budgetary and human resources dedicated to competition enforcement in Dominican Republic, including Pro-Competencia's budget (e.g., through governmental funding, administrative fees of a future merger control regime, and resources from international co-operation agreements, and avoid the use of sanctions for this purpose).

- Enable Pro-Competencia to prioritise enforcement and advocacy actions based transparent criteria (e.g., economic and geographic impact, relevance to consumers, public procurements or strategic industries), including the power not to take enforcement actions or to close investigations based on its priorities and/or availability of resources.

Competition law enforcement

- Adopt a general ex-ante merger control regime in line with OECD standards and international best practices.
- Increase enforcement actions against cartels and abuse of dominance cases:
    - Develop effective anti-cartel detection tools such as pro-active methods (e.g., economic filters and industry monitoring) and anonymous complaints.
    - Ensure that sanctions have sufficient deterrent effects. Maximum caps of fines should be based on flexible elements that allow to consider the specific circumstances of the cases and the markets affected in line with international standards.
- Improve the procedural framework for enforcement actions:
    - Expand the length of the statute of limitation in line with international practices.
    - Increase the timeline limitation to conduct investigations and/or allow for more flexibility regarding the extension or suspension of investigation deadlines.
    - Protect the investigation phase, for instance by allowing Pro-Competencia to publish non-confidential versions of the decision to initiate the investigation and the complaints (instead of the full version) after the opening of the formal investigations.
    - Streamline the procedure for requesting authorisations for dawn raids, ensuring that they can be directly requested by Pro-Competencia's Executive Directorate solely based on indications of anti-competitive infringements.
    - Introduce deterrent fines for failure to reply, late replies and the use of incomplete or misleading information regarding requests of information by Pro-Competencia.

Competition advocacy and institutional co-operation

- Ensure that co-ordination mechanisms between Pro-Competencia and the sector regulators with competition enforcement powers are effectively implemented, including the use the consultation mechanism provided for in the Competition Act regarding the adoption of competition infringement decisions and draft sector regulation. Proper channels of information sharing, staff exchanges, and joint working groups should also be implemented. In addition, ensure the existence of formal co-operation agreements between Pro-Competencia and all sector regulators with competition enforcement powers.
- Ensure that government entities, including sector regulators with competition enforcement powers, explain the reasons when choosing not to follow Pro-Competencia's non-binding opinions and recommendations.
- Empower another entity (for instance, Pro-Consumidor) with the enforcement of unfair competition practices. Alternatively, Pro-Competencia should limit its investigations related to unfair competition practices to those affecting the general public economic interest, freeing up resources to competition infringement investigations. In this case, co-operation with Pro-Consumidor, particularly in relation to unfair competition practices, should be strengthened.

1 Institutional and legal framework

This section will provide an overview of the institutional and legal framework of competition law in the Dominican Republic. After describing the main features of the country, it will analyse the origin of the Competition Act and its scope of application, as well as how Pro-Competencia is structured, including its internal set-up, resources, and staff. Finally, it will cover regulators with powers to enforce competition law within their sectors, as well as specificities related to the area of intellectual property (IP) rights.

1.1. Country context

The Dominican Republic is the second largest country in the Caribbean with a surface of 48 671 km2, and the third largest by population, with approximately 10.7 million people. It occupies the eastern two thirds of the island of Hispaniola, situated between Puerto Rico and Cuba. Haiti, an independent republic, covers the other third part of Hispaniola. The Dominican Republic is surrounded by the Atlantic Ocean to the north and the Caribbean Sea to the south. The Capital city, Santo Domingo, became the site of the first permanent European settlement in the Americas and the first seat of Spanish colonial rule in 1492. The Dominican Republic became an independent state on 27 February 1844.

The Dominican Republic is a representative democracy. The executive power is exercised by the government and the legislative power is vested in the bicameral National Congress, composed of the Chamber of Deputies and the Senate. The judiciary exercises its supervisory power independently from the executive and the legislature.

The Constitution of the Dominican Republic (*Constitución de la República Dominicana*) was promulgated on 6 November 1844 and amended 39 times since then. It consists of a preamble and fifteen titles, which are divided into chapters and sections comprising 277 articles, as well as twenty transitory provisions. The latest version of the Constitution dates back from 13 June 2015.

In the last decade, the Dominican Republic was the third fastest growing economy in Latin America and the Caribbean. Between 2013 and 2019, the country grew at an average annual rate of around 6% (IDB, 2021[1]). Economic expansion was largely driven by macroeconomic stability and a deeper integration in the global economy, with substantial foreign direct investment flows, the development of free trade zones[1] and the growth of tourism and mining (OECD, 2022[2]).

In 2022, GDP grew 4.9%, mainly driven by services. In particular, the tourism sector grew 24% in 2022, supported by an active government vaccination campaign during the Covid-19 pandemic, and a recovery in global tourism. Expansionary fiscal policy also contributed to growth (World Bank, 2023[3]).

Despite the strong and sustained economic growth and social improvements in the two last decades, the Dominican Republic still faces challenges related to poverty and inequality. For example, poverty was reduced between 2004 and 2019, but was aggravated due to the pandemic (Figure 1.1), even though the Dominican Republic has increased its capacity to protect the most vulnerable and strengthened social protection tools (OECD, 2022[2]).

Figure 1.1. Fast growth in income per capita vs. slow decline of poverty and inequality

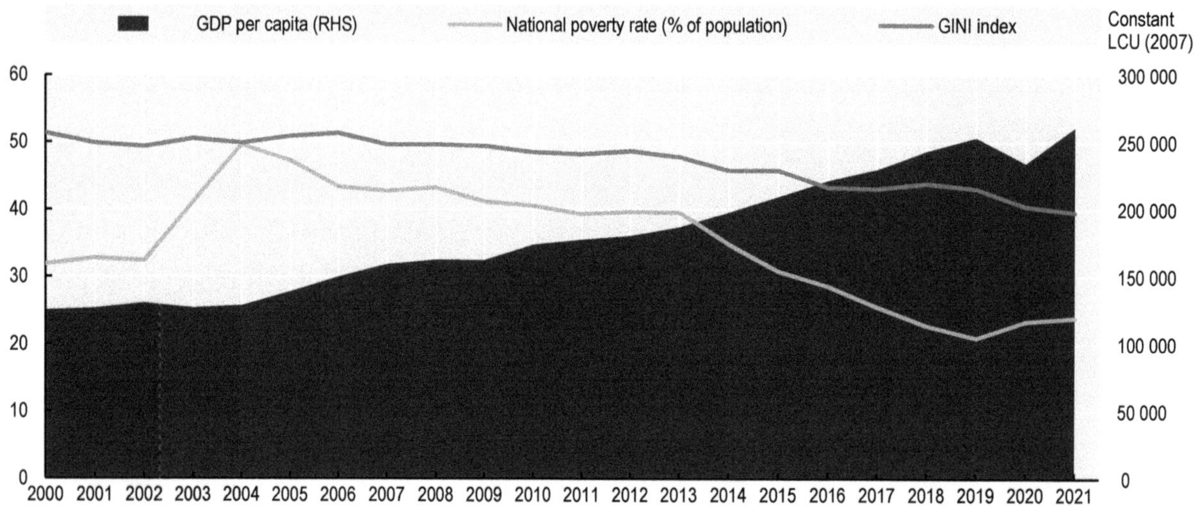

Note: Since 2016, the surveying methodology of the National Labour Force Survey changes to become the National Continuous Labour Force Survey, so poverty data may not be perfectly comparable before and after 2015. Estimates for GDP per capita from WEO April 2022, start after 2019, base year is 2007.
Source: Reproduced from OECD (2022[2]), Multi-dimensional Review of the Dominican Republic: Towards Greater Well-being for All, OECD Development Pathways, https://doi.org/10.1787/560c12bf-en.

Labour informality is also a critical and lasting challenge in the Dominican Republic. Informal employment rate was 59% in 2021, slightly above the average level observed in Latin America and the Caribbean of 56.5% (OECD, 2022[2]).

As in most economies worldwide, inflation is also a major challenge in the coming years. End-of-year inflation reached 7.8% in 2022, bypassing the Central Bank's target range of 4.1%. The cost of the family consumption basket increased 23.5% in 2022, compared to 2019, with the poorest being the most affected. To face price increases, the country has adopted subsidies for fuels, energy, transport, and basic food products, widening the fiscal deficit (World Bank, 2023[3]). Since the beginning of 2023, inflation has been reduced, and July's result (i.e. 3.95%) marked the lower rate since June 2020, within the Central Bank's target range (Banco Central de la República Dominicana, 2023[4]).

Moreover, trust in public institutions has been relatively low and volatile. Confidence in national government was particularly low in 2011 (41%), 2015 (45%) and 2019 (41%), but reached higher levels more recently, with 63% and 57% of the population having confidence in the government in 2020 and 2021, respectively. Current levels of confidence remain above the LAC (38%) and the OECD (47%) averages (OECD, 2022[2]).

Finally, the market concentration in the country is above the regional average, being more prominent in food processing industries, fuel production, constructions materials, as well as in the telecommunications, ports, domestic transport, electricity, and financial sectors (OECD, 2022[2]). As explained in Sections 1.5 and 2.1 below, competition law in some of these sectors is enforced by sector regulators and has not been effectively applied.

1.2. Origins and foundations

As in many other Latin American and Caribbean countries, free and fair competition is a constitutional right in the Dominican Republic, although the Dominican Constitution has an unusual provision that prohibits monopolies except for those established by law to benefit the state and protect the national security (Article 50 of Dominican Constitution). So far, legal monopolies have been established in the following areas: drinking water, sewage, radio spectrum, mining, postal service, electricity transmission and distribution, and highways. The State must encourage and ensure free and fair competition by adopting the necessary measures to prevent the harmful and restrictive effects of the legal monopolies and abuses of a dominant position. It should be noted that in practice the interpretation of this constitutional provision is that holding a monopoly (or dominant) position is not itself illegal and only its abuse can be sanctioned.[2]

Discussions on a draft competition act started in 1996 as part of a project to develop a Market Order Code (*Código de Ordenamiento del Mercado*), compiling rules on several economic areas, including competition. In 2005, after long and unsuccessful debates in Congress, the Executive Branch decided to extract the draft competition act from the Market Order Code and propose a stand-alone text. The Dominican Competition Act was finally adopted in 2008, providing for the creation of the Dominican competition authority, Pro-Competencia (National Commission for the Defence of Competition, *Comisión Nacional de Defensa de la Competencia*),[3] to be led by the Board of Directors (*Consejo Directivo*), the decision-making body, and the Executive Director (*Director Ejecutivo*), the head of the investigatory body. During the legislative process, some important elements of competition policy, particularly a merger control regime, were removed from the legal text (Pagán, 2017[5]).

Although the Competition Act has been enacted in 2008, Pro-Competencia's first Board of Directors was appointed in 2011. The first Executive Director was only appointed in 2017, when the Competition Act became fully operational, as per Article 67 of the Competition Act. Between 2011 and 2017, Pro-Competencia worked to prepare the institution for the fully operation of the Competition Act, focusing mostly on advocacy initiatives.[4] The first investigations against anti-competitive practices were launched by Pro-Competencia's in 2017 and the first competition infringement decision was issued in 2018.

The Dominican Competition Act focuses on the need for regulating the competitive process to achieve economic efficiency with the ultimate goal of protecting consumer welfare. The preambles of the Competition Act also refer to the competition regime as a condition for the Dominican Republic to be active in the globalised economy, as well as to be part of the Dominican Republic-Central America-United States Free Trade Agreement.[5]

On 15 June 2020, the government adopted the Implementing Regulation,[6] which details the procedures for the effective application of the Competition Act, in particular as regards Pro-Competencia's competition enforcement powers.

Competition policy is part of the Ministry of Economy, Planning and Development's Strategic Development Plan 2030, which includes among its initiatives the promotion of competition, aiming at reducing costs and prices, as well as raising the competitiveness of the Dominican economy (Ministerio de Economia, 2012[6]).

1.3. Scope of application

Article 3 of the Competition Act provides for a broad substantive scope of application (i.e. the persons and entities to whom the legislation is applied). Accordingly, competition law applies to all economic agents that carry out economic activities in the Dominican Republic (including legal entities, whether public or private, for- or non-profit, national or foreign, as well as individuals when directly developing economic activities). It also applies to trade associations, state-owned companies and state authorities. Moreover, competition law applies to individuals who have participated in anti-competitive practices, either directly, as accomplices or concealers, personally or as an employee, or on behalf of a legal entity.[7]

The Competition Act has also extra-territorial scope, applying to economic players that operate outside the Dominican territory if the effects of their behaviour restrict competition within the national territory.

Furthermore, the Competition Act establishes that it applies to the entire economy, but only as complementary law to economic agents regulated by sectoral laws with competition law provisions (Article 2). As further explained in section 1.5, specific legislations derogate from the general competition regime established by the Competition Act and provides for special regimes in the telecommunications, financial and banking, electricity and inland transport sectors, as well as for intellectual property rights.[8] In those cases, the competition enforcement powers have been granted to the respective regulators, and Pro-Competencia has no jurisdiction to apply competition law, but can engage in advocacy initiatives with the regulators (see section 3.1.1). In sum, certain sectors are subject to specific competition provisions, although the Competition Act remains applicable to fill the legal gaps of the specific competition regimes.[9]

Finally, there is no general competition merger control regime applied to the entire economy. Indeed, as will be discussed in section 2.1, the Competition Act does not establish a merger review system, although there exist certain merger control mechanisms enforced by regulators in the telecommunications, electricity, and financial sectors.

1.4. Pro-Competencia

As mentioned above, Pro-Competencia is the Dominican competition authority. It was created by the Competition Act in 2008 and became fully operational in 2017, as described in section 1.2.

Pro-Competencia is a decentralised and autonomous body, reporting to the Ministry of Industry, Commerce and SMEs. It is a legally independent entity, with legal status and administrative, budgetary, and organisational autonomy. Pro-Competencia has competition enforcement powers, including to conduct investigations and sanction anti-competitive agreements, abuses of dominant position and unfair competition practices. Furthermore, it is responsible for promoting competition within the Dominican Republic.

Competition enforcement of Pro-Competencia is still in its early stages. Since 2017 when it became fully operational, it had opened 14 investigations against anti-competitive practices[10] and adopted two competition infringement decisions (see Section 2.2).[11] In the advocacy front, Pro-Competencia has been more active both domestically and internationally (see Section 3.1).

1.4.1. Internal Structure

Like several other jurisdictions, the Dominican Republic has adopted an institutional model with a separation between adjudication and investigation functions (Jenny, 2016[7]; OECD, 2015[8]). The investigation function has been allocated to the Executive Directorate, while the decision-making power belongs to the Board of Directors.

The Executive Directorate's main task consists of receiving and responding to complaints and conducting investigations into possible anti-competitive and unfair competition practices. The Executive Directorate also carries out market studies, drafts opinions and organises advocacy activities. In addition, the Executive Director participates as a secretary in the meetings of the Board of Directors, drafts the minutes of the meetings and prepares the Board's draft administrative decisions.

In charge of investigations, the Executive Directorate is led by an Executive Director and composed of the following technical departments: (i) Competition Defence Unit, responsible for conducting the investigation phase and handling cases against anti-competitive and unfair competition conduct; (ii) Anti-Competitive Practices Investigations Unit, in charge of gathering evidence for the Competition Defence Unit by using the different investigations tools available, in particular dawn raids; (iii) Competition Advocacy and Promotion Unit, responsible for assessing the anti-competitive nature of national laws, state support measures, and acts of regulators, carrying out outreach activities and promoting competition in the country; (iv) Economic and Market Studies Unit, in charge of conducting market studies, providing support with economic expertise to the Competition Defence Unit, the Competition Advocacy and Promotion Unit and the Board of Directors, as well as carrying out the Observatory of Market Conditions (see section 3.1.2). In addition, the Financial Unit, the Legal Department[12] and the Planning and Development Unit provide administrative support to the Executive Directorate.

The Board of Directors' is composed of five Directors. Its main functions include adopting infringement decisions, after the investigation phase has been concluded, as well as conducting hearings of the investigated and affected parties, witnesses, and experts. Hearing and judgement sessions are public, as well as Pro-Competencia's infringement decisions.[13] The Board of Directors is also responsible for authorising the dawn raids organised by the Executive Directorate and requesting the adoption of interim measures to the competent courts (see Section 2.3). Moreover, the Board of Directors has the power to set internal rules,[14] as well as to promote competition before other government entities.[15] Decisions of the Board are adopted by simple majority and all Members of the Board are required to vote and must explain the legal grounds and the reasoning behind dissenting votes.[16]

To support the activities of the Board of Directors, in May 2023 the Technical Management Unit was established to provide assistance with the legal and economic analysis of the decisions to be taken by the Board.[17] The Board of Directors is also composed of the following support units: (i) Human Resources Unit; (ii) Institutional Relations Unit; (iii) Communications Unit; and (iv) IT Unit.

Figure 1.2. Pro-Competencia's organigram

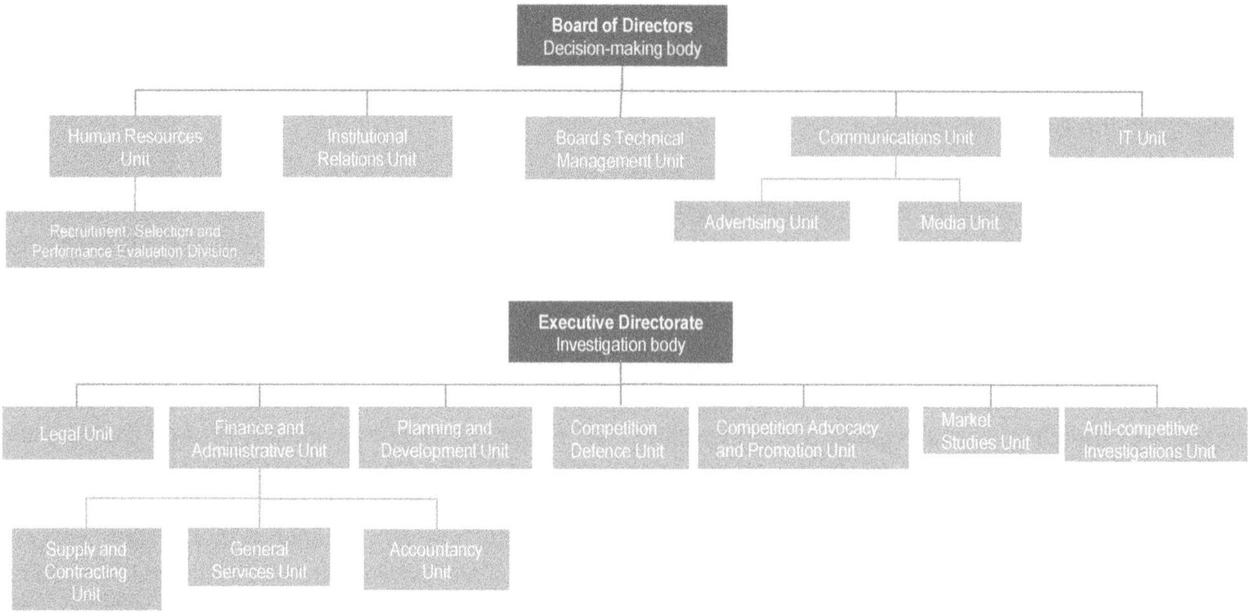

Note: This is a simplified organigram; the official version is available at www.procompetencia.gob.do/sobre-nosotros/organigrama/.
Source: Adapted from Pro-Competencia (2021[9]), Organigrama, https://procompetencia.gob.do/wp-content/uploads/2020/10/cd-010-2020-anexo.pdf; Pro-Competencia (2020[10]), Manual de Organización y Funciones de la Comisión Nacional de Defensa de la Competencia, https://procompetencia.gob.do/wp-content/uploads/2020/10/cd-010-2020-anexo.pdf; Pro-Competencia (2021[11]), Decision No. 014-2021 from 22 July 2021, https://procompetencia.gob.do/wp-content/uploads/2021/08/resolucion-014-2021-firmada-y-sellada.pdf.

1.4.2. Appointments and dismissals

The Board of Directors is composed of five members appointed for a non-renewable term of five years. Staggered rotation of Directors every three years allows for partial renewals and continuity within the Board. Members of the Board are appointed by the National Congress from a list of 10 candidates proposed by the President of the Dominican Republic. Three members are elected by the Senate and two by the Chamber of Deputies. The President of the Board of Directors is elected by its members.[18] The Executive Director is appointed by the President of the Dominican Republic from a list of three candidates proposed by the Board of Directors.[19]

Members of the Board of Directors and the Executive Director are required to meet the following eligibility criteria: (i) they must be Dominican national in possession of full civil and political rights; (ii) they must be over the age of 25; (iii) they must be a professional in law, economics, administrative sciences or finance, with specialised studies in any of the following disciplines: competition law, economic regulation, law and economics, corporate finance, alternative dispute resolution or international arbitration; (iv) they must have a credible experience of more than five years in any of the above areas or in the business practice; and, (v) they must not hold any position or employment of any nature while in office, with the exception of lecturing.[20]

Directors can only be removed if: (i) they have unjustifiably failed to attend six ordinary sessions per year; (ii) due to physical disability they have been unable to perform their duties for six months; (iii) they have been criminally convicted; (iv) they have been negligent in the performance of their duties; (v) they have committed fraud, illegal activities or have acted contrary to the objectives and interest of the institution.[21] The National Congress has the powers for any removal.[22]

The technical personnel at second and third management level are appointed and removed by the Board of Directors upon proposal of the Executive Director.[23]

1.4.3. Incompatibilities

According to Article 28 of the Competition Act, the following individuals may not be appointed as member of the Board of Directors or as Executive Director:

a) Members of the National Congress.
b) Active members of the Judicial Branch.
c) Those who hold remunerated positions or jobs in any of the agencies of the State or municipalities, whether by election or by appointment, except for lecturing.
d) Those with a family link (by blood up to the fourth degree or by affinity up to the second degree, inclusive) to the President or Vice President of the Dominican Republic, the members of the Supreme Court of Justice or directors of sector-specific regulators.
e) Those having an active political militancy.
f) Persons who have been declared in cessation of payment or in bankruptcy, as well as those against whom bankruptcy proceedings are pending.
g) Persons declared legally or judicially incapable; or
h) Persons who are in a situation of conflict of interest due to their professional or economic activities.

Conflict of interest has only been established as an impediment for members of the Board of Directors and the Executive Director and may be invoked either by them or the investigated parties. Cases of conflict of interest are decided by the Board of Directors.[24]

1.4.4. Resources

The proper functioning and independence of a competition authority rely on adequate staff and budget. While competition authorities worldwide face resource constraints in some form, it is necessary to ensure that the funds are used in the most efficient way (OECD, 2009[12]).

Budget

As mentioned above, Pro-Competencia has budgetary and spending autonomy.[25] Pro-Competencia is mainly financed by a budget line from the annual public budget of the government (*Presupuesto de Ingresos y Ley de Gastos Públicos*).[26] The annual budget of the competition authority is calculated by Pro-Competencia and authorised by the General Direction for Budget (*Dirección General de Prespuesto, Digepres*), the government entity overseeing the budget system processes, the quality and efficiency of spending, the fiscal sustainability and macroeconomic stability of the Dominican Republic. Pro-Competencia may also receive funds from administrative fees, resources from international technical co-operation (e.g. agreements with foreign countries or international organisations) and the sanctions imposed on economic agents. Budget expenditure is audited by the Comptroller General of the Dominican Republic (*Contraloría General de la República*).[27]

Pro-Competencia's budget for 2022 was approximately USD 3 million (DOP 167.4 million).[28] The budget has remained nearly the same since 2018 and was frozen in 2022 due to budgetary restrictions imposed by the government after the Covid-19 pandemic (see Figure 1.3).

Figure 1.3. Pro-Competencia's budget 2017-2022

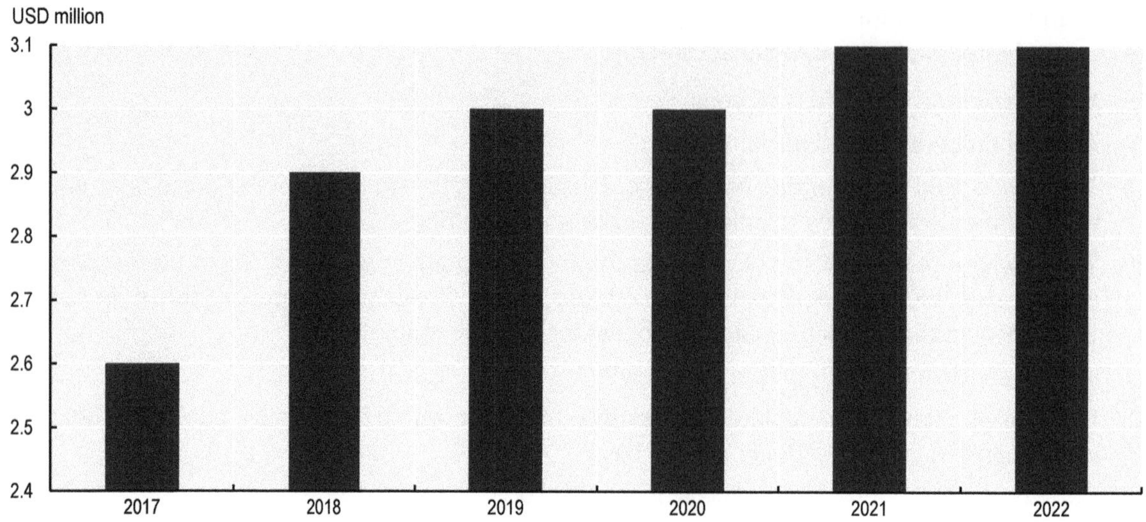

Source: OECD based on Pro-Competencia's data.

Pro-Competencia's budget is considerably low for international and regional standards. Figure 1.4 below compares Pro-Competencia's annual budget per capita for 2016 to 2021 with the budget per capita of certain groups of countries that provided data to the OECD CompStats Database,[29] in particular (i) OECD countries, (ii) countries in the Latin American region; (iii) countries with GDP per capita similar to the Dominican Republic; and (iv) countries with similar number of inhabitants to the Dominican Republic. Pro-Competencia's budget appear below in all these situations when compared to any of the indicated categories.

Figure 1.4. Budget per capita (2015 EUR exchange rate), 2016-2021

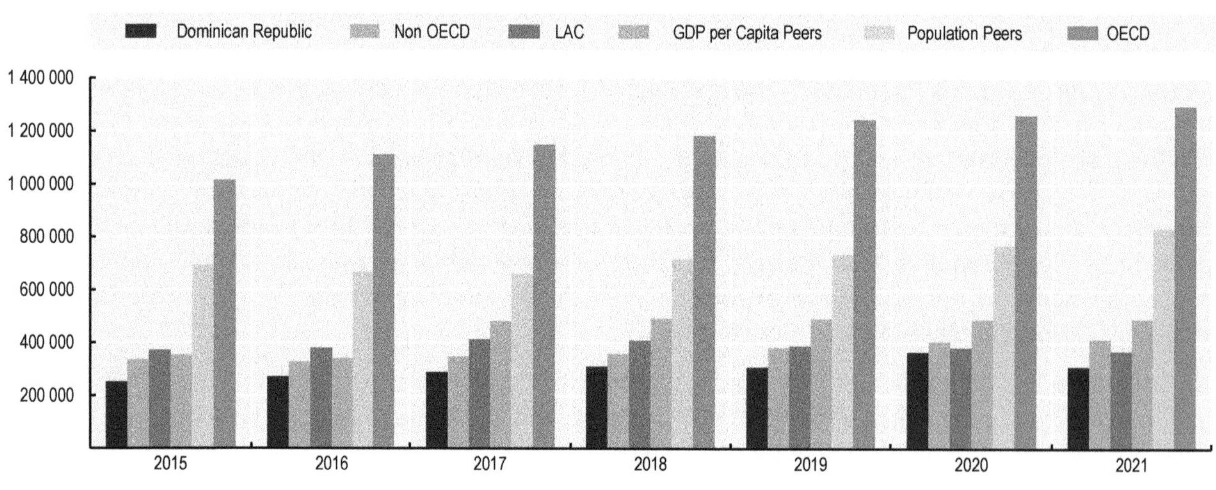

Note: The list of all jurisdictions participating in the OECD CompStats Database is available at OECD (2023[13]), OECD Competition Trends 2023, https://www.oecd-ilibrary.org/docserver/bcd8f8f8-en.pdf?expires=1687792175&id=id&accname=guest&checksum=081BCF39906154FA32F8AB6E61A464FA. GDP per Capita peers include jurisdictions that have a difference of less than EUR 3 500 vis-à-vis the Dominican Republic's GDP per Capita. Population peers include jurisdictions with a difference of less than 1.5 million inhabitants compared to the Dominican Republic's population.
Source: OECD (2023[14]), CompStats database, https://www.oecd.org/competition/oecd-competition-trends.htm.

An important part of Pro-Competencia's budget is allocated to salary expenses. In addition to human resources, Pro-Competencia's budget is spent on office space, technological devices and proprietary, licensed or purchased softwares. At the time of writing, economists at the authority had requested the purchase of powerful computers that are able to run sophisticated software for data analytics. Furthermore, Pro-Competencia did not have a digital case management system. The case file was on paper format and staff from the Competition Defence Unit spent many of their working hours registering, recording and scanning case documents. Pro-Competencia had not invested on IT forensics either.

At the time of writing, Pro-Competencia had never received funds from sanctions,[30] administrative fees or resources from international technical co-operation.[31]

Sources of funding which are not entirely dependent on the governments' discretion may help limit political interference and, thus, reinforce the authority's independence. As described above, in the Dominican Republic, such sources could be obtained through administrative fees (e.g. if a merger regime with filing fees is established), international technical co-operation and sanctions imposed on economic agents.

Relying entirely on these mechanisms, however, has limitations and may create other difficulties for the authorities. For instance, collecting and retaining (all or part of) the fines can be problematic as it may create perverse incentives for an agency to impose more fines (OECD, 2016[15]). The best approach is a combination of different sources of funding to reduce the risk of a single source.

Human resources

At the time of writing, Pro-Competencia's staff was made up of 70 full-time employees. However, only around a third (35%) were assigned to the authority's core competition activities; the rest (65%) were administrative support staff. Employees dedicated to substantive enforcement and advocacy work include: the 5 members of the Board of Directors; the Executive Director; and 19 technical staff working at the Competition Defence Unit, the Anti-Competitive Practices Investigations Unit, the Competition Advocacy and Promotion Unit and the Economic and Market Studies Unit. Except for those working at the Economic and Market Studies Unit, who have an economic and business administration background, the rest of the technical staff are lawyers. Investigations are led by lawyers with the support of economists who carry out the economic analysis of cases. Pro-Competencia has been progressively transforming administrative positions into technical ones. Indeed, the administrative support staff leaving the competition authority has not been replaced aiming to create new positions for competition activities.

The number of employees at Pro-Competencia is significantly lower than in other comparable jurisdictions, especially if support staff is not taken into account. As shown in Figure 1.5., the number of staff per million inhabitants for the years 2016 to 2021 in the Dominican Republic was lower than in: (i) OECD countries, (ii) countries in the Latin American and Caribbean region; (iii) countries with GDP per capita similar to the Dominican Republic; and (iv) countries with similar number of inhabitants to the Dominican Republic.

Figure 1.5. Number of staff per million inhabitants, 2016-2021

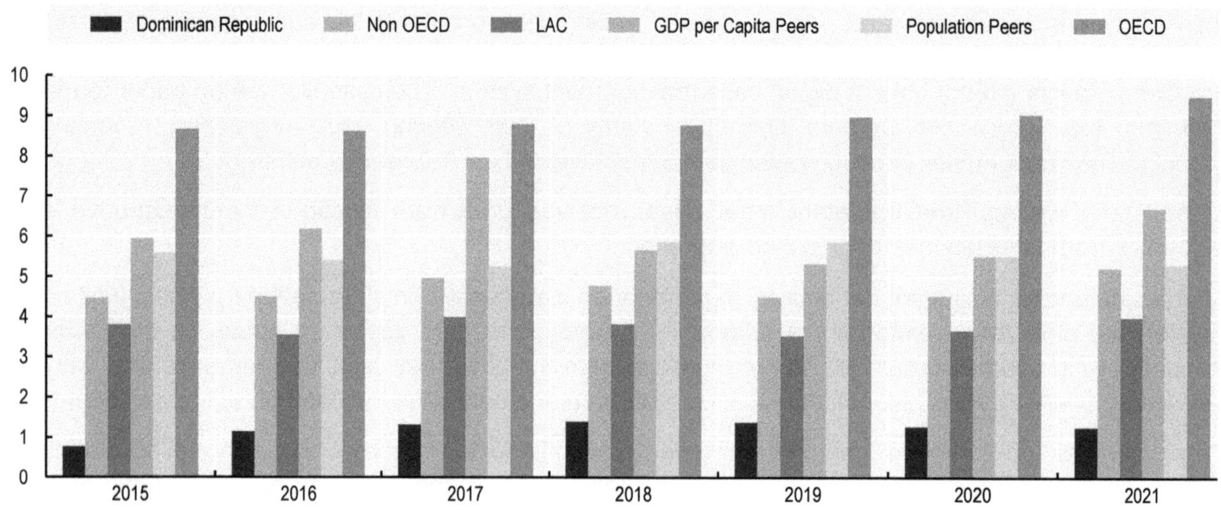

Note: The list of all jurisdictions participating in the OECD CompStats Database is available at OECD (2023[13]), OECD Competition Trends 2023, https://www.oecd-ilibrary.org/docserver/bcd8f8f8-en.pdf?expires=1687792175&id=id&accname=guest&checksum=081BCF39906154FA32F8AB6E61A464FA. GDP per Capita peers include jurisdictions that have a difference of less than EUR 3 500 vis-à-vis the Dominican Republic's GDP per Capita. Population peers include jurisdictions with a difference of less than 1.5 million inhabitants compared to the Dominican Republic's population.
Source: OECD (2023[14]), CompStats Database, https://www.oecd.org/competition/oecd-competition-trends.htm.

Except for the members of the Board of Directors and the Executive Director, employees at Pro-Competencia must go through a recruitment process carried out by the authority's Human Resources Unit. Staff can be hired: (i) as public officials or (ii) as employees under a temporary contract. All personnel are formally hired by the Board of Directors upon recommendation of the Executive Directorate.

Only public officials can be promoted. Promotions are granted based on criteria established by the Ministry of Public Administration (*Ministerio de Administración Pública*).[32] At the time of writing, from the total number of employees at Pro-Competencia (i.e. 70 workers), there were only 10 administrative public officials, the remaining staff being temporary employees.

Pro-Competencia has expressed the need to hire more technical staff to deliver its mandate. In fact, at the time of writing, there were 18 vacant positions for technical staff at Pro-Competencia. However, these vacancies could not be filled in because the budget was spent on other items and there were no resources available to hire additional staff.

Competition law and economics are highly technical, specialised fields. To attract and retain highly skilled, staff competitive salaries and fulfilling career paths matter. Indeed, the Competition Act requires that salaries at Pro-Competencia are competitive in relation to the private sector and at the same level as the average salaries offered at other decentralised bodies.[33] This, however, does not seem to be the case in practice. Salaries at Pro-Competencia are not as attractive as in the private sector and are lower than salaries offered for similar responsibility in some of the other government entities (see Table 1.1).

Table 1.1. Comparison of salaries of equivalent positions in different government entities

Type of position	Government entity/Monthly salary		
	Pro-Competencia	Dominican Institute of Telecommunications (INDOTEL)	Superintendency of Banks
Head of the entity	USD 9 100 (DOP 500 000) (President of the Board of Directors)	USD 9 387 (DOP 515 506) (President of the Board of Directors	USD 20 874 (DOP1,145,184) (Superintendent)
Members of the decision-making body	USD 7 595 (DOP 416 667) (Members of The Board of Directors)	USD 5 859 (DOP 321 463 (Members of The Board of Directors)	N/A
Head of investigation/supervision	USD 6 749 (DOP 370 000) (Executive Director)	USD 8 178 (DOP 448,494) (Executive Director)	USD 10 962 (DOP 601 240) (Submanager of supervision)
Chief economist	USD 3 463 (DOP 190 000) (Director of Market Studies Unit)	USD 3 682 (DOP 201 999) (Head of Economic Analysis)	USD 7 828 (DOP 429 458) (Director Dept. of Economic Studies)

Source: OECD based on Pro-Competencia's data.

Pro-Competencia's ability to increase salary offers for public officials is limited. The level of compensation is set by the government according to grade and scale. The competition authority needs a special authorisation from the Ministry of Public Administration (*Ministerio de Administración Pública*) and the General Directorate of Budget (*Dirección Nacional de Presupuesto*) to improve those salary conditions, which has never occurred in practice.

Pro-Competencia has more leeway regarding salaries of temporary staff, who are, in general, better paid than public officials. However, career development for temporary employees is uncertain as there are no clear rules regarding promotion opportunities. The turnover rate of employees at Pro-Competencia was 30% in 2022. Most technical staff have left the competition authority to work in law firms and other regulators offering better salaries.

1.4.5. Priority-setting

Strategic planning at Pro-competencia has been limited to its internal organisation. Every three years, Pro-Competencia carries out an evaluation and an internal consultation to set up its Institutional Strategic Plan (*Planificación Estrátegica Institucional*, PEI). This tool defines Pro-Competencia's objectives and establishes indicators and goals for their monitoring and evaluation. These objectives must be in line with the National Development Strategy (*Estrategia Nacional de Desarrollo*), which establishes the government's commitments, objectives and projects for the country in the next 20 years (Ministerio de Economia, 2012[6]).

Pro-Competencia's 2021-2024 PEI (Pro-Competencia, 2021[16]) identifies two strategic lines: i) the effective creation and promotion of a culture of competition among economic agents, the State and citizens; and ii) the strengthening and effective promotion of an organisational culture among Pro-Competencia's employees, fostering the sense of belonging through individual, group and leadership development.[34] As shown in Table 1.2, under each strategic line, Pro-Competencia identifies different objectives:

Table 1.2. Pro-Competencia's strategic lines and objectives

Strategic line 1. Create and promote a culture of competition	Strategic line 2. Strengthen and promote organisational culture within the authority
Objective 1.1. Strengthen competition enforcement tools for the detection of anti-competitive practices and instruction of procedures.	Objective 2.1. Complete the structural needs of human resources for the promotion of institutional identity and belonging.
Objective 1.2. Raise competition awareness of key groups through active participation in the national agenda.	Objective 2.2. Improve the working environment to improve work performance and institutional activities.
Objective 1.3. Design, develop and promote economic analysis and competition intelligence reports.	Objective 2.3. Strengthen technical and cross-cutting capabilities in leadership management and target occupational groups through development programs.
Objective 1.4. Promotion of inter-institutional technical assistance on competition issues.	

Source: OECD based on Pro-Competencia (2021[16]), Plan Estrategico Institucional 2021-2024, https://procompetencia.gob.do/transparencia/plan-estrategico-institucional/#44-45-wpfd-planificacion-estrategica-institucional.

Indicators to measure the attainment of those objectives are based on the number of actions undertaken. For example, the indicator to measure whether Pro-Competencia has met objective 1.1 (i.e. strengthen competition enforcement tools for the detection of anti-competitive practices and instruction of procedures) is the number of investigations rejected in relation to the number of investigations opened.

The Competition Act does not allow Pro-Competencia to set its own priorities regarding enforcement actions, namely as regards the complaints received. Indeed, the authority is required to investigate, at least preliminarily, all complaints and cannot reject them based on priority grounds.[35] The lack of clear priorities is also favouring a trend within Pro-Competencia to be reactive rather than proactive in its ex-officio investigations (see section 2.4.1). In fact, investigations are often opened in response to news in the media or a punctual government action. This affects the investigations team's case-planning, which often has to suspend on-going investigations to focus on the new urgent cases. According to some stakeholders, this reactive approach has negatively impacted the effectiveness of competition enforcement in the Dominican Republic.

The large amount of complaints competition authorities receive can create a heavy workload. For that reason, it is relevant that competition authorities are able to decide which cases will be investigated and which cases can be dropped based on pre-established priorities. The level of discretion enjoyed by competition authorities in setting priorities varies from one jurisdiction to another. Likewise, the criteria used by competition authorities to set priorities diverge. Some examples of those criteria include: the nature of the case, the geographic impact, the relevance of the evidence, the importance of the sector affected by the infringement, the size of the market or if the claim deals with a novel issue or a new type of infringement. Overall, competition authorities set their priorities focusing on strategically important sectors from a competition law perspective. Other public interests and the views of other public institutions may be taken into consideration during the priority-setting process, but competition authorities safeguard the right to set its own criteria independently (OECD, 2015[17]).

Box 1.1. Prioritisation criteria for competition enforcement and advocacy in Mexico

Every three years, the Mexican Federal Economic Competition Commission (Comisión Federal de Competencia Económica, COFECE), makes public its priority-setting criteria and the economic sectors and areas it will prioritise.

Thanks to the priority-setting exercise, COFECE can focus the use of resources on actions that produce impactful results rendering its operations more effective.

COFECE's 2022-2025 Strategic Plan sets the following criteria for prioritisation of competition work: (i) contribution to economic growth; (ii) generalised consumption; (iii) transversality; (iv) impact on lower-income population; (v) regulated sectors; (vi) prevalence of anti-competitive conducts; and (vii) international trends in competition matters.

By applying these criteria, COFECE has identified eight priority sectors for 2022-2025: (i) food and beverages sector; (ii) transport and logistics sector; (iii) financial sector; (iv) construction and real-estate services sector; (v) energy sector; (vi) health sector; (vii) public procurement; and (viii) digital markets.

COFECE also promotes accountability of its priority-setting agenda, by being transparent on the criteria used for this purpose and submitting its Strategic Plan for public consultation, which allows relevant stakeholders to participate in the priority setting process.

Source: COFECE (2022[18]), Strategic Plan 2022-2025, https://www.cofece.mx/wp-content/uploads/2022/11/PE2022-2025-ing-VF.pdf.

1.5. Regulators with competition powers

As previously mentioned, a few specific legislations establish their own competition law provisions, derogating some sectors (i.e. telecommunications, electricity, financial and banking, as well as inland transport) and intellectual property rights from the general competition law regime.

However, the way specific competition provisions were drafted are divergent, resulting in a patchwork of different competition regimes, with different sets of competition rules. For instance, while some of them only prohibit unfair competition practices, others also cover anti-competitive behaviour and/or ex-ante merger control. The powers to enforce those competition provisions have been granted to the respective regulators, who shall apply the Competition Act as a complementary law to fill the gaps of the specific competition regimes.[36] Pro-Competencia has no jurisdiction to apply competition law in relation to conducts taking place in these sectors, although it may be consulted and issue non-binding opinions to sector regulators in relation to their competition enforcement actions (see section 3.1.1).

The institutional set-up of the Dominican Republic can deliver some benefits (e.g. it may allow the regulators to use a variety of tools to address a competition concern and foster a competition culture in sector regulation), but it raises a number of challenges, such as the risk of inconsistent enforcement of competition law across different sectors, legal uncertainty and duplication of resources to develop competition policy expertise in each sector regulator. For those reasons, this model is unusual in OECD countries. Indeed, the most widespread institutional model is the one where the competition authority is a stand-alone agency with responsibilities for applying competition in all sectors, which ensure a uniform approach to competition enforcement throughout the economy and reduce the risk of regulatory capture (OECD, 2022[19]).

In addition, certain stakeholders in the Dominican Republic have expressed concerns during the fact-finding mission about possible conflicting interests between sector regulation and competition enforcement, as well as the lack of competition expertise within some regulatory entities that have the powers to enforce competition law.

Co-ordination between the competition authority and the sector regulators enforcing competition provisions is regulated by the Competition Act. As further explained in Section 3.2.1, the Competition Act requires Pro-Competencia and the regulators to jointly establish a competition framework that will apply uniformly across all sectors with specific competition regimes. Nevertheless, the deadline to finalise this common competition framework (i.e. 2019) was never met.[37] Instead of developing this uniform competition regime, Pro-Competencia and the sector regulators have signed bilateral institutional agreements aiming at: (i) regulating the consultation mechanism about competition enforcement actions provided for in Article 20 of the Competition Act; (ii) setting the framework for the exchange of information; and (iii) adopting joint capacity building initiatives (see Section 3.2.1).

1.5.1. Telecommunications sector

The General Telecommunications Law (*Ley General de Telecomunicaciones*, LGT) regulates the telecommunications sector in the Dominican Republic.[38] The LGT created the Dominican Institute of Telecommunications (*Instituto Dominicano de las Telecomunicaciones*, INDOTEL), an autonomous and decentralised entity in charge of overseeing the telecommunications sector. The decision-making body of INDOTEL, the Board of Directors, consist of five members appointed by the President of the Dominican Republic (i.e. the President; the Minister of Economy, Planning and Development; two representatives of the regulated undertakings, being one representing the broadcasters and another representing the telecommunications service providers; and one representative of the end users). The Executive Director of INDOTEL, the authority in charge of investigations, also participates in the discussions of the Executive Board without voting rights. The presence of regulated agents' representatives (i.e. broadcasters and telecommunication service providers) in the governing body of INDOTEL may facilitate policy capture compromising the independence of the institution.

INDOTEL is responsible for (i) promoting the development of the telecommunications infrastructure and services in the country through the implementation of the universal service principle; (ii) ensuring effective competition in the telecommunications markets; (iii) protecting consumer and end-users' rights; and (iv) warranting the efficient use of the radio spectrum.

INDOTEL ensures effective competition in the sector as a sector regulator, by adopting regulation to establish and protect fair and free competition in the telecommunications market (ex-ante regulatory intervention).[39] Furthermore, INDOTEL also operates as a competition authority, (i) controlling mergers prior to their implementation (ex-ante competition intervention) and (ii) sanctioning anti-competitive and unfair competition practices (ex-post competition intervention).[40]

In 2005, INDOTEL adopted a regulation to establish more detailed procedures for the enforcement of competition law in in the telecommunications sector (INDOTEL Competition Regulation).[41]

INDOTEL has enforcement powers in relation to both unfair competition practices and anti-competitive conduct. According to the LGT, unfair competition practice is all deliberate action aimed at harming or eliminating competitors, misleading the end user and/or gaining an unfair advantage. Unfair competition practice includes misleading or false advertising; denigration of competitors' products or services; industrial bribery; violation of trade secrets; or acquisition of sensitive information by non-legitimate means.[42]

Anti-competitive practices are defined by the LGT and the INDOTEL Competition Regulation as agreements between companies or abuses of dominant position that could restrict or distort free competition in all or part of the national telecommunications market, to the detriment of suppliers and end users. The following conducts are listed in the LGT as anti-competitive practices:[43]

a) Discriminatory practices against third parties;

b) Limitation and impediment of the users' right to freely choose the telecommunications provider;
c) Abuse of market power, in particular regarding essential infrastructures;
d) Predatory practices that tend to impair or effectively limit sustainable, fair and effective competition;
e) Refusal to negotiate in good faith or unjustifiably delaying negotiations.

This is a non-exhaustive list, and INDOTEL can investigate and sanction other anti-competitive practices not listed in the LGT. Anti-competitive conducts are considered as a very serious infringement by the LGT and can be sanctioned with a fine of up to approximately USD 373 000. However, this is lower than the maximum fine provided for in the Competition Act, based on the weighted average minimum wage (i.e. USD 954 000), as discussed in Section 2.4.5.[44]

As further explained in Section 2.1.1, INDOTEL is also in charge of reviewing mergers and acquisitions in the telecommunications sector.

In addition, INDOTEL can conduct, *ex officio* or at the request of an interested party, market studies to assess the competition conditions of the telecommunications markets. The purpose of the market studies is to detect barriers to entry, abuses of dominant position and unfair competition practices.[45]

The Unit in charge of investigating anti-competitive and unfair competition conduct in INDOTEL is composed of three lawyers and two economists. Since 1998, INDOTEL has only adopted one enforcement decision related to competition law (see Box 1.2 below) and approved two mergers with conditions (see Section 2.1.1) (INDOTEL, 2016[20]; 2017[21]; 2017[22]). At the time of writing, INDOTEL had conducted one market study related to competition issues.[46]

Box 1.2. Cable TV operators' case

In 2004, INDOTEL sanctioned 23 cable TV operators for having broadcasted content without the authorisation of the authors. According to INDOTEL, this conduct violated the Copyright Law No. 65-00 and the general principles of fair competition provided for in the LGT.

INDOTEL considered that the wrongdoing violated general competition law principles because other cable operators that had complied with the Copyright Law, obtained authorisation, and paid royalties to authors were operating under disadvantageous conditions.

According to INDOTEL, cable TV operators' misbehaviour constituted a minor infringement of the LGT, and each economic agent was sanctioned to pay a fine of approximately USD 1 300 (DOP 72 000).

Source: INDOTEL (2004[23]), Decision No. 012-04 of 30 January 2004, https://transparencia.indotel.gob.do/wp-content/uploads/2022/10/resolucion-no-012-04.pdf.

1.5.2. Electricity sector

The General Electricity Law (*Ley General de Electricidad*, LGE)[47] and its implementing regulation[48] govern the electricity market in the Dominican Republic. The LGE creates two governing bodies: the National Energy Commission (*Comisión Nacional de Energia*, CNE) and the Superintendency of Electricity (*Superintendencia de Electricidad*, SE).

The CNE reports to the Executive branch through the Ministry of Energy and is responsible for advising the government in relation to energy markets, preparing and co-ordinating the drafting of legal and regulatory texts, as well as proposing and adopting energy policies and standards. The SE, the sector regulator, reports to the CNE, supporting the latter in the implementation and attainment of its policy objectives, for instance by set prices subject to regulation, monitoring compliance with regulation and sanctioning those who do not follow regulation.

The CNE is composed of a Board of Directors (i.e. Minister of Industry, Commerce and SMEs, Minister of the Presidency, Minister of Finance, Minister of Agriculture, Minister of Environment and Natural Resources, Governor of the Central Bank and Director of INDOTEL) and an Executive Director, appointed by the President of the Dominican Republic.[49] The SE consists of a President (also known as Superintendent of Electricity) and two members, appointed by the President of the Dominican Republic following the National Congress approval.[50]

In the Dominican Republic, the distribution and commercialisation of electricity are state legal monopolies, and their prices are regulated by SE. The electricity generation is the only activity in the energy sector that has been liberalised. The long-term sale of electricity to distributors are subject to public procurement and should follow the prices established therein.[51] Electricity generation companies with long term contracts with distributors must sell 40% of their production in the spot market.[52] Competition law enforcement in the electricity sector is in the remit of the CNE and the SE and is limited to the liberalised activity (i.e. electricity generation).

The LGE establishes that the CNE must ensure the proper functioning of the markets in the electricity sector and avoid monopolistic practices in the liberalised sector.[53] The SE monitors the behaviour of the economic agents in order to avoid monopolistic practices, and sanctions those that infringes the LGE.[54]

According to the LGE, a monopolistic practice is any action that has as its object or effect the prevention, restriction or distortion of competition within the electricity market, for instance fixing of the purchase or sale prices or other transaction conditions; limiting or controlling the energy production; allocating markets; or applying unequal conditions to third parties for equivalent services.[55]

Monopolistic practices are considered as very serious infringements under the LGE and can be sanctioned with a fine of up to almost USD 2 million and USD 4 million in case of recidivism. These numbers are higher than the maximum fine provided for in the Competition Act (i.e. USD 954 000).[56]

Neither the LGE nor its implementing regulation establish a procedure to monitor or investigate potential anti-competitive practices. At the time of writing, no significant experience in enforcing competition law by the SE was identified.

The LGE and the implementing Electricity Regulation set up a mandatory notification system to monitor economic concentrations in the electricity sector (see Section 2.1.2).

1.5.3. Financial and banking sector

The financial and banking sector is regulated by the Monetary and Financial Law (*Ley Monetaria y Financiera*, LMF),[57] which created the governing bodies of the monetary and financial system of the Dominican Republic: the Central Bank (*Banco Central*), the Monetary Board (*Junta Monetaria*) and the Superintendency of Banks (*Superintendencia de Bancos*). The Central Bank is at the top of the Dominican financial and banking system and oversees the monetary policy, acting as bank to the Government and other bankers and monitoring the domestic banking system. The Monetary Board sets up the concrete monetary and financial policies of the Dominican Republic. The Superintendency of Banks monitors the activity of the financial intermediation entities and their compliance with the relevant regulation.

The Monetary Board consists of 3 ex officio members (the Governor of the Central Bank, the Minister of Finance and the Superintendent of Banks) and 6 members appointed by the President of the Dominican Republic.[58] The Central Bank is led by a Governor (appointed by the President of the Dominican Republic), with the support of an Executive Committee.[59] The Superintendency of Banks is led by a Superintendent, appointed by the President of the Dominican Republic.[60]

As discussed in Section 2.1.3, the Monetary Board, upon proposal of the Superintendency of Banks, reviews mergers and acquisitions between financial intermediation entities. However, the merger review in these cases does not analyse the competition effects of the transaction, but rather focuses on other aspects, such as financial stability, digitalisation and innovation, financial inclusion, institutional efficiency and strength, consumer protection and integrity of the financial system.

The Superintendency of Banks can also investigate and sanction financial intermediation entities for engaging in misleading advertising or unfair competition practices. Sanctions for such conducts include fines of up to approximately USD 45 500 (DOP 2 500 000).[61] No relevant experience in this regard had been identified at the time of writing.

Anti-competitive conduct in the financial sector, such as horizontal or vertical agreements and abuses of dominant position, fall outside the scope of the LMF and could, therefore, be investigated by Pro-Competencia. However, at the time of writing, Pro-Competencia had not taken any competition enforcement or advocacy initiative in this sector.

1.5.4. Inland transport sector

The inland transport sector is regulated by the Law on Mobility, Land Transport, Traffic and Road Safety (*Ley de Movilidad, Transporte Terrestre, Tránsito y Seguridad Vial*, the "Inland Transport Law").[62] The Inland Transport Law created the National Institute of Inland Transport (*Instituto Nacional de Tránsito y Transporte Terrestre*, INTRANT), led by an Executive Director, appointed by the President of the Dominican Republic.[63] The INTRANT is in charge of managing mobility, inland public and private transport, and road safety in the Dominican Republic. It is also responsible for fighting against monopolistic practices and market dominance in the sector, ensuring market entry, as well as contributing to market transparency by publishing statistics and information about prices, demand and supply.[64]

Despite having competition enforcement powers within the inland transport sector, the INTRANT does not have a unit or team dedicated to investigating anti-competitive practices. Since its creation, INTRANT has not launched any investigation or adopted any sanctioning decision against anti-competitive practices.

1.5.5. Intellectual property rights

Industrial Property in the Dominican Republic is regulated by the Industrial Property Law (*Ley de Propiedad Industrial*, LPI).[65] The National Office of Industrial Property (*Oficina Nacional de la Propiedad Industrial*, ONAPI) is the institution responsible for enforcing the LPI and ensuring the protection of inventions by managing Industrial Property (IP) rights. ONAPI is under the direction of a Directorate, composed of five members (Minister of Industry, Commerce and SMEs, Minister of the Presidency, Ministry of Public Health and Social Assistance, Ministry of Culture and Education and Director of the Dominican Institute for Industrial Technology), who appoints a General Director, in charge of leading the institution.[66]

ONAPI has also competition enforcement powers, which includes ensuring that IP licensing contracts do not contain anti-competitive clauses[67] and granting compulsory licenses where it has determined that the patent owner had engaged in anti-competitive practices.[68] According to the LPI, anti-competitive practices consist of: (i) setting the prices of the patented products at an excessive or discriminatory level; (ii) licensing IP rights under unreasonable commercial terms; (iii) using IP rights to limit the commercial or productive activities of the licensee; and (iv) any other action that the national legislation qualifies as anti-competitive conduct.[69]

Thus, provisions of the Competition Act defining concerted practices and agreements, as well as abuses of dominant position, should be enforced by ONAPI if they relate to IP rights, regardless of the sector in which the practices occur.

In addition, the LPI refers to unfair competition practices, which are similar to the provisions of the Competition Act. Some of the unfair competition practices contained in the LPI include the misuse of designation of origin,[70] commercial or professional acts contrary to honest customs and practices;[71] misuse of distinctive elements of an undertaking causing confusion or risk of association; and use of denigrating statements.[72] According to the LPI, the competent authority to deal with unfair practices related to IP rights is the judicial authority, and ONAPI has no enforcement function therein.[73]

Main findings

The main findings on the institutional and legal framework of competition law and policy in the Dominican Republic include:

- The competition law framework includes a general competition law regime (enforced by Pro-Competencia) and sector-specific competition law regimes (enforced by key sector regulators). The existing legal framework is not always consistent, resulting in a patchwork of different competition rules applicable throughout the economy.
- Absence of a wide competition merger control regime applied to the entire economy, although certain merger control mechanisms exist in the telecommunications, electricity and financial sectors (only the telecommunications regulator analyses the competition effects of the transactions, while the electricity and financial sectors focus on regulatory aspects).
- Pro-Competencia's annual budget is considerably low for international and regional standards. Pro-Competencia's staff is also lower than comparable jurisdictions and only a third of its employees are assigned to competition activities (and the rest work in other activities mainly administrative support).

References

Banco Central de la República Dominicana (2023), *Precios*, https://www.bancentral.gov.do/a/d/2534-precios (accessed on 17 August 2023). [4]

COFECE (2022), "Strategic Plan 2022-2025", https://www.cofece.mx/strategic-plan-2022-2025/. [18]

IDB (2021), *Dominican Republic, IDB Group Country Strategy 2021-2024*. [1]

INDOTEL (2017), "Decision No. 056-17", https://transparencia.indotel.gob.do/wp-content/uploads/2022/10/res-no-056-17.pdf. [21]

INDOTEL (2017), "Decision No. 077-17", https://transparencia.indotel.gob.do/wp-content/uploads/2022/10/res-077-17-fusion-altice-recurso-de-reconsideracion-contra-la-056-17.pdf. [22]

INDOTEL (2016), "Resolución No. 001-16", https://transparencia.indotel.gob.do/wp-content/uploads/2022/10/resolucion-no-001-16.pdf. [20]

INDOTEL (2004), "Decision No. 012-04", https://transparencia.indotel.gob.do/wp-content/uploads/2022/10/resolucion-no-012-04.pdf. [23]

Jenny, F. (2016), "The Institutional Design of Competition Authorities: Debates and Trends", https://doi.org/10.2139/ssrn.2894893. [7]

Ministerio de Economia, P. (2012), "Ley 1-12: Plan Estratégico de Desarrollo 2030", https://mepyd.gob.do/mepyd/wp-content/uploads/archivos/end/marco-legal/ley-estrategia-nacional-de-desarrollo.pdf. [6]

OECD (2023), *OECD Competition Trends 2023*, https://www.oecd.org/competition/oecd-competition-trends.htm. [13]

OECD (2023), *OECD Services Trade Restrictiveness Index: Policy trends up to 2023*, OECD Publishing, https://www.oecd.org/trade/topics/services-trade/. [14]

OECD (2022), "Interactions between competition authorities and sector regulators: OECD Competition Policy Roundtable Background Note", https://www.oecd.org/competition/interactions-between-competition-authorities-and-sector-regulators.htm. [19]

OECD (2022), *Multi-dimensional Review of the Dominican Republic: Towards Greater Well-being for All, OECD Development Pathways*, OECD Publishing, https://doi.org/10.1787/560c12bf-en. [2]

OECD (2016), *Participation in Global Value Chains in Latin America: Implications for Trade and Trade-Related Policy, Working Party of the Trade Committee*, https://www.oecd.org/officialdocuments/publicdisplaydocumentpdf/?cote=TAD/TC/WP(2015)28/FINAL&docLanguage=En. [15]

OECD (2015), *OECD Review of the Corporate Governance of State-Owned Enterprises: Lithuania*, https://www.oecd.org/daf/ca/Lithuania_SOE_Review.pdf. [17]

OECD (2015), *Summary Record: Annex to the Summary Record of the 123rd Meeting of the Competition Committee held on 15-19 June 2015. Key points of the Roundtables on Changes in Institutional Design*, OECD Publishing, https://one.oecd.org/document/DAF/COMP/M(2015)1/ANN9/FINAL/En/pdf. [8]

OECD (2009), "OECD Global Forum on Competition: Challenges Faced by Young Competition Authorities", https://www.oecd.org/daf/competition/GFC2009-Challenges-faced-by-young-competition-authorities.pdf. [12]

Pagán, A. (2017), "Origen de la Ley de Defensa a la Competencia de la República Dominicana", https://lalibrecompetencia.com/2017/01/17/origen-de-la-ley-de-defensa-a-la-competencia-de-la-republica-dominicana-1-de-2/. [5]

Pro-Competencia (2021), "Plan Estratégico Institucional 2021-2024", https://procompetencia.gob.do/transparencia/plan-estrategico-institucional/#44-45-wpfd-planificacion-estrategica-institucional. [16]

Pro-Competencia (2021), *Decision No. 014-2021 from 22 July 2021*, https://procompetencia.gob.do/wp-content/uploads/2021/08/resolucion-014-2021-firmada-y-sellada.pdf. [11]

Pro-Competencia (2021), "Organigrama", https://procompetencia.gob.do/sobre-nosotros/organigrama/. [9]

Pro-Competencia (2020), *Manual de Organización y Funciones de la Comisión Nacional de Defensa de la Competencia*, https://procompetencia.gob.do/wp-content/uploads/2020/10/cd-010-2020-anexo.pdf. [10]

World Bank (2023), *Macro Poverty Outlook for Dominican Republic : April 2023 (English)*, https://thedocs.worldbank.org/en/doc/e408a7e21ba62d843bdd90dc37e61b57-0500032021/related/mpo-dom.pdf. [3]

Notes

[1] For instance, the Dominican Republic is part of the Dominican Republic-Central America-United States Free Trade Agreement (CAFTA-DR) and the CARIFORUM-EU Economic Partnership Agreement.

[2] See Article 50, item 1 of the Dominican Constitution and Article 7, paragraph IV of the Competition Act.

[3] General Law for the Defence of Competition No. 42-08 (*Ley No. 42-08 sobre la Defensa de la Competencia*) of 16 January 2008, https://www.micm.gob.do/images/pdf/transparencia/base-legal-de-la-institucion/leyes/Ley_No._42-08_Sobre_la_Defensa_de_la_Competencia.pdf. The Dominican Constitutional Court has assessed Article 50 of the Dominican Constitution on some occasions, e.g. Decisions No. TC/0267/13 (19 December 2013) and No. TC/0137/20 (13 May 2020).

[4] For instance, Pro-Competencia has issued guidelines and carried out market studies (see section 3.1). In 2012, Pro-Competencia has also hosted the 10th meeting of the IDB/OECD Latin American and Caribbean Competition Forum (LACCF).

[5] The Dominican Republic-Central America-United States Free Trade Agreement (CAFTA-DR) encompasses the United States, Costa Rica, El Salvador, Guatemala, Honduras, Nicaragua, and the Dominican Republic.

[6] Regulation No. 252-20 implementing the Competition Act (*Reglamento No. 252-20 de aplicación de la Ley General de Denfensa de la Competencia)* of 15 July 2020, https://micm.gob.do/images/pdf/transparencia/base-legal-de-la-institucion/resoluciones/decretos/2020/Decreto-252-20.pdf.

[7] Article 60, paragraph I of the Competition Act.

[8] Article 69 of the Competition Act and Article 16, sole paragraph of the Implementing Regulation also mention other regulated sectors: energy, hydrocarbons, air and maritime transport, health, education, insurance, pension and stock market), but according to Pro-Competencia their sectoral legislations do not have provisions related to competition law enforcement.

[9] Article 2 of the Competition Act.

[10] Moreover, Pro-Compentencia has opened a number of investigations against unfair competition practices.

[11] In addition, Pro-Competencia has sanctioned a legal entity for providing the Executive Directorate with false information during an investigation (Decision No. 001-2022 from 4 January 2022, https://procompetencia.gob.do/resoluciones-procompetencia/resolucion-numero-001-2022/).

[12] Article 34 of the Competition Act.

[13] Articles 47, 48 and 50, sole paragraph of the Competition Act.

[14] Article 31, item "j" of the Competition Act.

[15] Articles 14, 15 and 31, item "n" of the Competition Act.

[16] Article 50 of the Competition Act.

[17] Decision No 014-2021, from 22 July 2021, https://procompetencia.gob.do/wp-content/uploads/2021/08/resolucion-014-2021-firmada-y-sellada.pdf.

[18] Article 26 of the Competition Act.

[19] Article 33 of the Competition Act.

[20] Articles 27 and 34, paragraph II of the Competition Act.

[21] Article 29 of the Competition Act.

[22] Article 83, item 1 of the Dominican Constitution.

[23] Article 31, "y" of the Competition Act.

[24] Article 39 of the Implementing Regulation.

[25] Article 16 of the Competition Act.

[26] Article 21 of the Competition Act.

[27] Article 16 of the Competition Act.

[28] Conversion made on 19 April 2023.

[29] The OECD CompStats database compiles general statistics relating to 79 jurisdictions, including the Dominican Republic. Information of CompStats database is compiled in the publication OECD Competition Trends (OECD, 2023[13]).

[30] Although Pro-Competencia has already sanctioned three cases, the funds from the fines will only be transferred to Pro-Competencia when there is a final judicial ruling confirming the administrative decision, which had not yet occurred at the time of writing.

[31] Nevertheless, Pro-Competencia has benefited from technical co-operation provided by foreign jurisdictions or international organisations, such as the United States Authority for International Development (USAID), the European Union and the Inter-American Development Bank.

[32] Decision 230-2021 of the Ministry of Public Administration (*Ministerio de Administración Pública*) establishes the criteria for considering an institutional promotion, including (i) having obtained "Above Average" or "Outstanding" performance evaluation in at least the last two consecutive evaluations; (ii) not having been subject to disciplinary sanctions in the last two years; (iii) not being subject to any disciplinary process pending decision; and (iv) having completed the required training programs.

[33] Article 22 of the Competition Act.

[34] At the time of writing, Pro-Competencia was developing the Institutional Strategic Plan for 2024-2027, with the support of the European Union through a technical co-operation agreement.

[35] Articles 36, 37 and 38 of the Competition Act.

[36] Articles 2 and 20 of the Competition Act.

[37] Article 69 of the Competition Act.

[38] Ley General de Telecomunicaciones (LGT) No. 153/98 of 15 April 1998, https://transparencia.indotel.gob.do/wp-content/uploads/2022/10/ley-no-153-98.pdf.

[39] Article 92.1 of LGT.

[40] Articles 1 and 8 of LGT and Chapter IV of the Regulation of fair and free competition for the public telecommunication services, adopted by Decision No. 022-05, https://transparencia.indotel.gob.do/wp-content/uploads/2022/10/36-resolucion-no-022-05-actualizada-con-derogaciones-modf-078-19.pdf.

[41] Regulation of fair and free competition for the public telecommunication services, adopted by Decision No. 022-05.

[42] Article 1 of the LGT.

[43] Article 8 of the LGT.

[44] This is equivalent to 200 times the charge for infringement (*cargo por incumplimiento*) in 2021, which equals DOP 21 424 400. See Article 109 of the LGT.

[45] Article 18 of Regulation of fair and free competition for the public telecommunication services, adopted by Decision No. 022-05.

[46] Decision No. 047-2020 from 29 July 2020, https://www.indotel.gob.do/wp-content/uploads/2022/10/res_signed_047-2020_estudios_consultoria_cowi_signed.pdf.

[47] Ley General de Electricidad No. 125-01, https://www.sie.gob.do/images/sie-documentos-pdf/leyes/LeyGeneraldeElecctricidadNo.125-01.pdf.

[48] Reglamento para la aplicación de la Ley General de Electricidad 125-01 aprobado por Decreto No. 555-02 https://www.cne.gob.do/wp-content/uploads/2015/05/Reglamento.Ley_.No_.125-01.pdf.

[49] Articles 16 and 18 of LGE.

[50] Article 31 of LGE.

[51] Article 110 of LGE and Article 44 of the implementing regulation.

[52] Article 44 of the implementing regulation.

[53] Item "e" of Article 14 of the LGE.

[54] Item "d" of Article 24 of the LGE.

[55] Article 2 of the LGE.

[56] Articles 126-1, item "c", and 126-4 of the LGE.

[57] Ley Monetaria y Financiera No. 183-02 del 21 de noviembre del 2002, https://sb.gob.do/media/c3hhtvb1/ley-no-183-02-monetaria-y-financiera.pdf.

[58] Articles 10 and 11 of the LMF.

[59] Article 17 of the LMF.

[60] Article 21 of the LMF.

[61] See Article 68, paragraph B, item 7 of the LMF and Articles 6 and 18 of the Sanctions Regulation of the Monetary Board (Reglamento de Sanciones Administración Monetaria y Financiera Junta Monetaria), https://www.sb.gob.do/media/hjybfkcn/reglamento-de-sanciones.pdf.

[62] Ley No. 63-17, de Movilidad, Transporte Terrestre, Tránsito y Seguridad Vial de la República Dominicana. G. O. No. 10875 del 24 de febrero de 2017, https://intrant.gob.do/phocadownload/SobreNosotros/MarcoLegal/Leyes/MARCO%20LEGAL-LEY%2063-17%20SOBRE%20TRANSITO,%20TRANSPORTE,%20Y%20SEGURIDAD%20VIAL.pdf.

[63] Article 13 of the Inland Transport Law.

[64] Article 9 and 10 of the Inland Transport Law.

[65] Ley de Propiedad Industrial No. 20-00, https://www.aduanas.gob.do/media/2214/20-00_sobre_propiedad_industrial.pdf.

[66] Articles 141 and 143 of the LPI.

[67] Article 33 of the LPI.

[68] Articles 42 and 43 of the LPI.

[69] Ibid.

[70] Article 133, number 1 of the LPI.

[71] Article 176.1 of the LPI.

[72] Article 177 of the LPI.

[73] Article 182 of the LPI.

2 Competition law enforcement

This section will cover key dimensions of competition law enforcement, including merger control in specific sectors of the economy, anti-competitive practices, investigation powers, sanctions, as well as judicial review and civil damage claims.

2.1. Merger control

As mentioned in Section 1.2, the first version of the draft Competition Act in Dominican Republic included a general competition merger control system, which was later removed from the bill of law and its final version. Thus, the Competition Act was adopted without a merger review system.

Companies and business associations have strongly pushed back the adoption of merger control in the Dominican Republic. They argue that merger control is not adapted to small economies, such as the Dominican, and that concentration is a natural consequence of the insular condition of the country. The business sector is particularly concerned about too many concentrations and acquisitions being blocked by the competition authority.

Effective merger review, which helps avoiding economic concentrations in general, is a key component of almost all competition regimes, independently of their size or condition. Business concerns about a great number of transactions being blocked is not founded. Merger control targets transactions that significantly reduce competition and causes consumer harm. Most of the mergers are authorised by competition authorities because they do not cause harm to competition and will often generate efficiencies. A minority of transactions may create competition problems and will require a thorough analysis and intervention from the competition authority (e.g., imposition of a remedy or the prohibition of the transaction) (OECD, 2021[1])

Almost all jurisdictions in the world have some form of merger control regime, assessing mergers' competitive impact on their relevant markets (OECD, 2021[1]). Indeed, from the 79 jurisdictions included in the OECD CompStats database in 2023, only seven had no regulatory framework for merger control in place (OECD, 2023[2]). All Dominican Republic's GDP per capita peers and population peers mentioned in Figure 4 and Figure 5 have a merger control regime.

This is also the case in Latin America and the Caribbean, where jurisdictions often have had first a competition law (without merger control) and left the introduction of merger control provisions to a subsequent stage of the development of competition law enforcement as indicated in Figure below. In fact, from the 14 jurisdictions in Latin American and the Caribbean included in the OECD CompStats database, only the Dominican Republic did not have a merger control regime. The other jurisdictions are: Argentina, Barbados, Brazil, Chile, Colombia, Costa Rica, Ecuador, El Salvador, Mexico, Nicaragua, Panama, Paraguay and Peru (OECD, 2023[2]).

Figure 2.1. Development of competition law and merger control regimes in Latin America and Caribbean

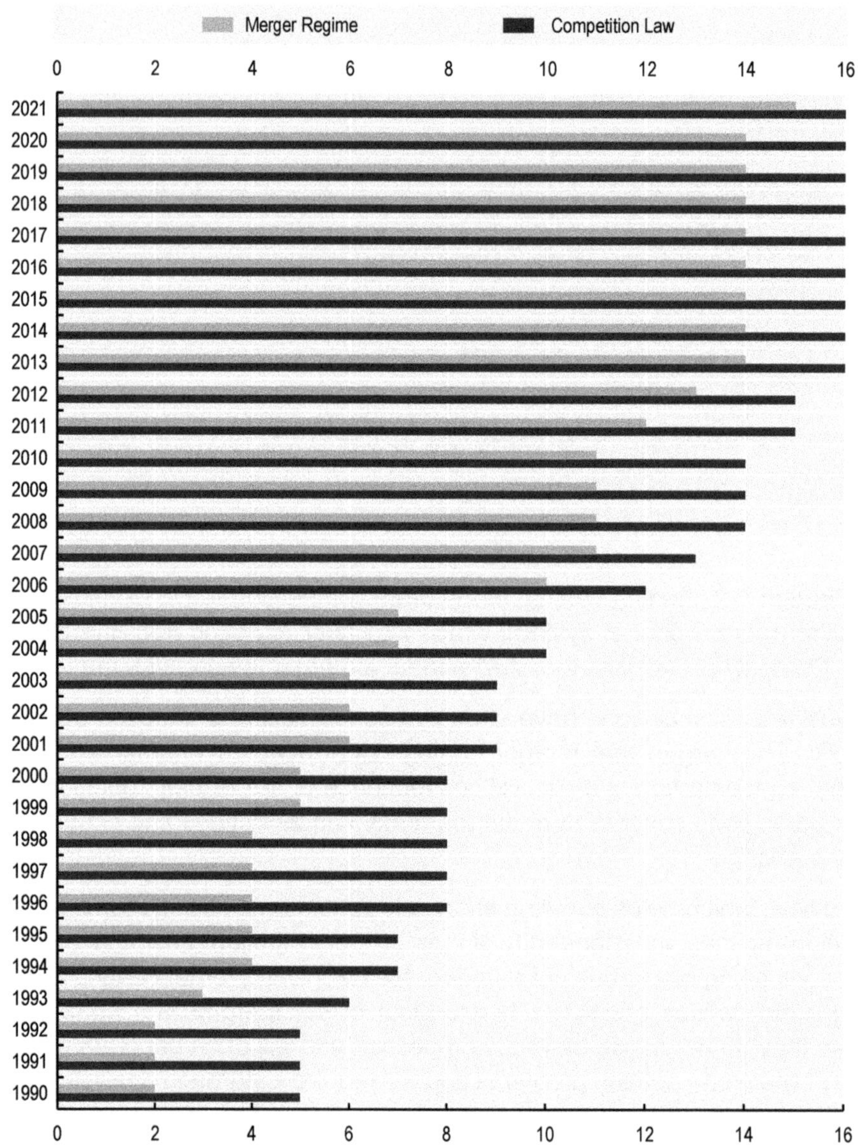

Note: in horizontal axis are the number or jurisdictions in LAC that had merger regime and competition law by the year in vertical axis.
Source: OECD (2023[2]), CompStats database, https://www.oecd.org/competition/oecd-competition-trends.htm.

In this context, the Dominican Republic still lacks a general merger control regime in order to follow common international practices and OECD guidance on this matter. Indeed, most jurisdictions recognise that competition problems of a structural nature may result from certain merger transactions, which justifies the existence of merger control provisions that help preventing market structures from excessive concentration and related competition issues.

In Latin America, Peru has recently adopted a mandatory merger control regime applied to the entire economy following a recommendation of the OECD-IDB Peer Review of the Competition Law and Policy in Peru (OECD-IDB, 2018[3]). The new Peruvian merger control legislation entered into effect in June 2021 and has resulted in 29 merger notifications in its first two years in force: 24 transactions have been authorised; 1 transaction has been withdrawn by the merging parties; and 1 transaction has been approved with restrictions in the pharmaceutical sector. No transactions have been blocked.

Indeed, the OECD Recommendation on Merger Review recognises the important role that an effective merger review plays within competition regimes, which contributes to greater convergence of merger review procedures, including co-operation among competition authorities, towards internationally recognised best practices. It also helps competition authorities and merging parties to avoid unnecessary costs by making merger review procedures more effective (OECD, 2005[4]).

While the Dominican Republic does not have a wide competition merger control regime applied to the entire economy, it has certain mechanisms resembling to merger control, not always based on competition rationale, that can be enforced by regulators in the telecommunications, electricity, and financial sectors. Overall, Pro-Competencia has not played any role in these review assessments, although such mechanisms could potentially benefit from greater interaction with competition experts (e.g., non-binding opinions by Pro-Competencia).

2.1.1. Telecommunications sector

The Dominican Institute of Telecommunications (*Instituto Dominicano de las Telecomunicaciones*, INDOTEL) is in charge of reviewing mergers and acquisitions in the telecommunications sector.[1] Prior notification of mergers and acquisitions among telecommunication companies is mandatory in the Dominican Republic and non-compliance may be sanctioned with a fine of up to approximately USD 390 thousand (DOP 21.4 million).[2] There are no merger notification thresholds in place.

INDOTEL may authorise without conditions, authorise with conditions, or prohibit a merger after having conducted an analysis of its effects on the relevant markets. The reasons for objecting to a merger are the unreasonable lessening, restriction, harm and impediment of free competition.[3] This may be the case, for example, if the merger confers the power for the new entity to restrict substantially the supply of products or services.[4]

INDOTEL has not been very active in this area. Since 2005, two mergers were authorised with conditions by INDOTEL. The example below indicates the most recent case involving companies Altice Hisponiola S.A. and Tricom S.A., which was conditionally approved by INDOTEL in 2017.

Box 2.1. Merger Altice/Tricom approved with conditions by INDOTEL, 2017

On 20 September 2017, INDOTEL, the Dominican telecommunications regulator, authorised with conditions the acquisition of the telecommunications operator Tricom S.A. by Alttice Hispaniola S.A.

The merger included the transfer of the authorisations granted to Tricom S.A. for the use of the radio electric spectrum segments. INDOTEL concluded that the accumulation of spectrum was going to lessen competition in the relevant markets for mobile telephony services and internet access. To address the negative competitive effects of the merger, INDOTEL imposed conditions including (i) granting back to the regulator certain frequencies previously assigned to Tricom S.A.; and (ii) obligations in relation to interconnection prices (e.g., obligation for Altice Hispaniola S.A. to publish its Reference Interconnection Offer – RIO).

On 22 November 2017, INDOTEL adopted a revised decision which considered requests received from both merging parties and one of their main competitors (i.e. Compañía Dominicana de Teléfonos, S. A. – CLARO) as regards INDOTEL's first decision on this case. As a result, additional obligations were included in the remedy package, e.g., the obligation to adopt a 3-year investment plan of at least USD 11.4 million (DOP 625 million) to deploy infrastructure to expand the coverage of mobile services with broadband capacity in the following underserved provinces in the Dominican Republic: Barahona, Bahoruco, Dajabón, Elías Piña and Pedernales.

Source: INDOTEL (2017[5]), Decision No. 056-17, https://transparencia.indotel.gob.do/wp-content/uploads/2022/10/res-no-056-17.pdf; INDOTEL (2017[6]), Decision No. 077-17, https://transparencia.indotel.gob.do/wp-content/uploads/2022/10/res-no-056-17.pdf.

Pro-Competencia is usually not involved in merger review in the telecommunications sector, although it may be consulted and issue advocacy opinions. As further explained in section 3.1.1, advocacy recommendations issued by Pro-Competencia are not binding, but INDOTEL is required to provide a justification when it decides not to follow such recommendations, even though this does not seem to occur in practice.

2.1.2. Electricity sector

The Superintendency of Electricity (*Superintendencia de Electricidad*, SE) is in charge of enforcing several regulatory provisions of the electricity legal framework in the Dominican Republic. SE is also in charge of investigating mergers, namely when there are changes in the control of other energy companies.

Indeed, the Dominican legislation establishes a mandatory merger notification system to monitor concentrations in the electricity sector, in which energy companies have to notify their shareholding composition twice a year and economic agents may address complaints to SE if they observe changes in the control of other energy companies as per Article 11 of the 2001 General Electricity Law (*Ley General de Electricidad*, LGE)[5] and Articles 10 and 11 of its implementing Electricity Regulation (*Reglamento para la aplicación de la Ley General de Electricidad*).[6]

The SE reviews all transactions leading to a concentration and is expected to block any deal resulting in vertical integration (i.e., those deals that would create entities active in more than one of the regulated markets, namely generation, distribution and commercialisation).[7] Vertical integration in the electricity sector is forbidden in the Dominican Republic, except for the three companies resulting from the capitalisation process of the electricity distribution market that was launched in the country in 2001 – which nevertheless must not hold more than a 15% market-share in the national electricity generation market.[8]

Since 2001, the National Energy Commission (*Comisión Nacional de Energia*, CNE), the national regulator for the electricity sector, had only adopted one decision ordering the divestiture of the generation activity of one energy company, AES Corporation Ltd., for exceeding the maximum market share allowed in the energy generation market for companies resulting from the capitalisation process of the electricity market. Although the decision had mainly a regulatory nature (i.e., to enforce a regulatory provision that prohibits players to participate in both generation and distribution markets with high market-shares), it developed competition arguments since SE stated that the existence of players with strong market power would have "(i) increased collusive practices; (ii) encouraged parallel conduct; and/or (iii) increased the tendency of oligopolies and excluded mavericks".[9]

In sum, the procedure to monitor shareholding composition in the electricity sector is very different from a traditional merger assessment carried out by competition authorities in other jurisdictions, in particular because the rationale of the analysis is not based on typical competition grounds but rather on a regulatory requirement (i.e. the prohibition of vertical integration).

2.1.3. Financial sector

Mergers and acquisitions between financial intermediation entities are reviewed by the Monetary Board (*Junta Monetaria*), body in charge of designing the monetary policy in the Dominican Republic, which will benefit from a mandatory and previous opinion to be issued by the Superintendency of Banks (*Superintendencia de Bancos*), the body in charge of monitoring the banking sector.[10]

The merger control assessment focus on the strategic objectives of the Superintendency of Banks, which include financial stability, digitalisation and innovation, financial inclusion, institutional efficiency and strength, consumer protection, as well as integrity of the financial system. In other words, competition issues do not play a role in the current framework of merger review in the financial sector (and Pro-Competencia is not required to play any role either). This seems at least inconsistent with the guidance provided in Article 2 of the Monetary and Financial Law that establishes that the regulation of the financial sector should ensure the well-functioning of the system in an environment of competitiveness, efficiency and free market.

Given that competition does not play a role in current merger review mechanism in the financial sector, the pertinent competition case law enforcement is still inexistant at this moment.

2.2. Types of infringements

In the area of anti-competitive practices, the Competition Act identifies two main categories of antitrust infringements: collusive practices between competitors (Article 5 of the Competition Act) and abuse of dominant position (Article 6 of the Competition Act). In addition, unfair competition practices are also established as an infringement in the Competition Act (Article 10 of Competition Act) and may be sanctioned by Pro-Competencia or directly by civil courts.

2.2.1. Collusive practices

The infringement related to collusive practices is established in Article 5 of the Competition Act:

> *Art. 5. The practices, acts and agreements between competing economic agents, whether express or tacit, written or verbal, which have as their object or which produce or may produce the effect of unjustifiably imposing barriers on the market, are prohibited. The following conducts are included within concerted practices and anti-competitive agreements:*
>
> *a) Agreeing on prices, discounts, extraordinary charges, other conditions of sale and the exchange of information having the same object or effect;*

> *b) Agreeing or co-ordinating bids or abstention from bids, tenders and public auctions;*
>
> *c) To allocate, distribute or assign segments or parts of a market of goods and services, indicating specific time or space, suppliers and clients;*
>
> *d) Limit the production, distribution or commercialisation of goods; or render and/or frequency of services, regardless of their nature; and,*
>
> *e) Eliminate competitors from the market or limit their access to it, from their position as buyers or sellers of certain products.*

Article 5 of the Competition Act covers a list of anti-competitive horizontal agreements, including: (i) price fixing; (ii) bid-rigging; (iii) market allocation; (iv) output restrictions; and (v) boycotts. However, the legal provision uses the following wording of "unjustified barriers" as a core element of the text: "which have as their object or which produce or may produce the effect of unjustifiably imposing barriers on the market, are prohibited" (underlined for this report). This language is not common in other jurisdictions and may limit in practice the prosecution of certain anti-competitive practices. In fact, most competition laws ban conducts that have as their object or effect the restriction, impediment or limitation of competition in the market, which is a broader concept than the imposition of unjustified market barriers. While market barriers play an important role for the competition assessment of certain cases, they have limited utility for the analysis of other cases (e.g., price-fixing agreements, which are considered a *per se* infringement in most competition law regimes).

In the Dominican Republic, collusive agreements are considered as per se infringements, following a decision issued by Pro-Competencia in 2021, in which it was stated that such practices presumably produce negative effects and therefore there is no need to examine their effects on the market.[11]

Nevertheless, Article 7, item 1 of the Competition Act provides for an exemption from the general prohibition of collusive agreements when such practices are accessory or complementary to an agreed integration or association that has been adopted to achieve greater efficiency of the productive activity or to promote innovation or productive investment. The application of such exemption must be requested by the investigated parties, who have the burden to prove the economic efficiencies of their behaviour.[12]

According to Pro-Competencia's 2021 decision, the anti-competitive effects of an agreement may be outweighed by economic efficiencies if a decision of Pro-Competencia justifies this exemption. This exception may apply only if: (i) the agreement contribute to improving the production, commercialisation and/or distribution of goods and services, or promoting economic or technical progress; (ii) consumers benefit from the efficiencies produced by the agreement; (iii) the restrictions are indispensable and strictly necessary to obtain the benefits derived from the agreement; and (iv) the agreement does not eliminate all competition.[13] This is similar to the exemption provided for in Article 101, item 3 of the Treaty on the Functioning of the European Union.

Anti-cartel enforcement is still incipient in the Dominican Republic. Since 2017, when Pro-Competencia began its enforcement activities, it has investigated seven cases in relation to horizontal agreements, which led to one sanction of a cartel in the pharmaceutical sector. Four cases were dismissed and two are still ongoing. In addition, the sector regulators with competition enforcement powers have not been active in this area either, and no sanctions were identified at the time of writing (see section 1.5).

Box 2.2. Cartel case in the pharmaceutical sector

In 2021, Pro-Competencia sanctioned Profarma Internacional, Sued & Fargesa, J. Gassó Gassó, and Mercantil Farmacéutica, all distributors of Glaxosmithkline (GSK) pharmaceuticals in the Dominican Republic, for having participated in a cartel, with total fines of around EUR 200 thousand (DOP 14 million).

The firms agreed on maximum rebates, prohibited discounts to downstream merchants, and agreed to apply prices recommended by GSK during 2015-2018. E-mails and documents were used as evidence of the concerted practices, which indicated that firms met in Sued & Fargesa headquarters to discuss the collusive conducts.

Despite considering the cartel-like conduct as a *per se* violation of the Competition Act, Pro-Competencia assessed the efficiency defence arguments presented by the defendants and concluded that the exemption provided for in Article 7, Item 1 of the Competition act was not applicable because the evidence submitted failed to prove any pro-competitive effects.

Pro-Competencia identified an overprice of 2% in the affected markets and the fines were calculated based on that estimation.

This decision was appealed by the defendants and upheld by the Superior Administrative Court (TSA), which concluded that Pro-Competencia had presented enough direct evidence to prove the involvement of the sanctioned parties in the cartel scheme. TSA's decision was appealed before the Supreme Court of Justice and a final decision was still pending at the time of writing.

Source: Pro-Competencia (2021[7]), Decisión No. 010-2021, https://procompetencia.gob.do/wp-content/uploads/2021/06/resolucion-num-010-2021-version-publica.pdf; Decisions No. 0030-02-2023-SSEN-00389 and No 0030-1643-2023-SSEN-00506 of the TSA.

No bid-rigging cases have been sanctioned and only two cases are currently ongoing, which seems a very low figure for usual enforcement standards in the region. The ongoing case relates to an alleged cartel in the procurement of canteen service and was triggered by a complaint from Low-Cost Canteens of the Dominican State (*Comedores Económicos del Estado Dominicano*), a public entity in charge of providing canteen services to low-income individuals. This indicates the importance of close co-operation between competition authorities and entities in charge of public procurements (see section 3.2.3**3.2.3**).

Furthermore, Article 5 of the Competition Act only refers to agreements between competing economic agents. Anti-competitive vertical agreements between undertakings active at different levels of the supply chain are not covered by the Competition Act. However, as in other jurisdictions in the Latin American and Caribbean region,[14] anti-competitive vertical restraints can be caught under the Competition Act if they are imposed unilaterally by a dominant company as part of an abuse of dominant position (see section 2.2.2).

2.2.2. Abuse of dominant position

Article 6 of the Competition Act on abuse of dominant position provides that:

> *Art. 6. Conduct that constitutes an abuse of the dominant position of economic agents in a relevant market susceptible of creating unjustified barriers to third parties is prohibited. Abuses of dominant position include the following conducts:*
>
> *a) Subordinating the decision to sell to the buyer to refrain from purchasing or distributing products or services of other competing companies;*

> *b) The imposition by the supplier of prices and other conditions of sale to its resellers, without there being a commercial reason that justifies it;*
>
> *c) The sale or other transaction conditioned to the acquisition or provision of an additional good or service, different or distinguishable from the main one;*
>
> *d) The sale or other transaction subject to the condition of not contracting services, acquiring, selling or providing goods produced, distributed or marketed by a third party;*
>
> *e) The refusal to sell or provide, to a certain economic agent, goods and services that are usually and normally available or offered to third parties; and when there are no alternative suppliers in the relevant market available and willing to sell under normal conditions. Exceptions are those actions of refusal to negotiate, on the part of the economic agent, when there is a breach of contractual obligations by the client or potential client, or when the commercial history of the client or potential client shows a high rate of returns or damaged goods, or lack of payment, or any other similar commercial reason;*
>
> *f) The application, in commercial or service relations, of unequal conditions for equivalent services, which place some competitors in a disadvantageous situation with respect to others without there being any commercial reason to justify it.*

Similar to the legal provision related to collusion, the abuse of dominance provision also relies on the on notion of unjustified barriers (i.e., "susceptible of creating unjustified barriers to third parties"), while most jurisdictions adopt an approach based on effects on competition, which is a broader concept. Therefore, abuses that restrict competition but do not create barriers to third parties would not be considered an anti-competitive infringement. Following international practices, abuse of dominance is assessed under the rule of reason, meaning that a behaviour will only be considered illegal if its anti-competitive effects outweigh its pro-competitive effects (economic efficiencies).[15]

Article 6 of the Competition Act provides a non-exhaustive list of abusive practices, which are commonly known under competition law such as: (i) exclusive dealing; (ii) resale price maintenance; (iii) tying; (iv) exclusive dealing; (v) refusal to supply; and (vi) discrimination. While vertical restraints are not explicitly mentioned in the list, the legal provision seems sufficiently broad to cover this practice – and the evolution of case law in future years may be useful to confirm or not this assumption. Indeed, vertical restraints are often covered by abuse of dominance provisions in Latin America, namely when the practice is imposed unilaterally by a dominant firm and results on negative effects on the market.[16]

The Competition Act also has a specific provision that establishes the legal criteria of what should be considered dominance for purposes of antitrust enforcement. It generally follows common standards, stating that Pro-Competencia must consider the market barriers; the power to set prices unilaterally or substantially restrict supply; market shares the ability to access other sources of inputs; and the relationship between firms in terms of competition and recent commercial behaviours.[17]

The Competition Act does not address exploitative abuses (such as excessive prices) that negatively affect consumers. Unlawful conduct is defined solely in terms of exclusionary practices that foreclose, by imposing barriers, competitors or other firms in the market.

In addition, the Competition Act provides that unilateral conduct may be justified if its pro-competitive effects (i.e., economic efficiencies) outweigh its anti-competitive effects (Article 7, item 2 of Competition Act). This is commonly known as "efficiency defence" or "rule of reason" in other jurisdictions. Pro-Competencia has the burden of proof in demonstrating the anti-competitive effects of the practice, while the investigated firms have the burden of proof in showing possible efficiencies.

Fighting against abuse of dominance practices is also in its infancy in the Dominican Republic. Pro-Competencia has investigated seven abuse of dominance cases since 2017, when it began its enforcement track-record, which led to one administrative sanction in the beer market (still pending of judicial review). Five cases were dismissed, while one case is still ongoing. The sector regulators with competition enforcement powers have not been active in this area either (see section 1.5).

Box 2.3. Abuse of dominance in the beer market

In 2018, Pro-Competencia imposed a USD 842,000 (DOP 46 million) fine against *Cerveceria Nacional Dominicana* (CND) for abusing its dominant position in the national beer market.

The investigation was launched in 2017 following a market study published by Pro-Competencia regarding competition in the beer market after CND was acquired in 2012 by AmBev, a major player in the beverage sector in Latin America.

The relevant market was defined as the production, commercialisation and distribution of beer in the national territory of the Dominican Republic. With a market share of over 98%, CND held a dominant position in that market, while United Brands, the main competitor in the national beer market, only held a market share of around 1.5%.

In 2018, Pro-Competencia adopted a decision establishing that CND infringed competition law by (i) imposing barriers to entry to new players; (ii) imposing resale prices; and (iii) imposing exclusivity clauses on distributors and clients. Amongst other practices, CND was discouraging retailers from selling brands from competitors, as well as imposing exclusive resale clauses for clients which prevented other beer suppliers to access consumers (e.g., exclusivity to cover promotion materials).

Pro-Competencia's decision was annulled by the Superior Administrative Court, since the market study used to prove the anti-competitive practice could not have been used as evidence. Pro-Competencia appealed to the Supreme Court of Justice and a final judicial decision was still pending at the time of writing.

Source: Pro-Competencia (2018[8]), Decision No. 018-2018, https://procompetencia.gob.do/resoluciones-procompetencia/resolucion-num-018-2018/; Decision No. Judgement No. 0030-04-2022-SSEN-02218 of the TSA.

2.3. Procedural issues

2.3.1. Investigative phase

The procedural steps that the Executive Directorate must follow are established in Article 44 of the Competition Act and Article 21 of the Implementing Regulation and must be carried out within 12 months (see section 2.3.3 below). First, the alleged offending parties must be notified of the opening of a formal investigation, informing the objections raised against them.[18] Then, the investigated parties have an extendable period of 20 working days to reply to the allegations and present evidence. Within this period, they may also offer commitments (see section 2.4.5). The period for submitting evidence is, however, not limited to the 20 working-days period as the investigated parties may bring forward further evidence anytime during the investigation procedure. This means that the investigated parties could submit evidence at the very end of this phase, and the Executive Directorate would not have the time to analyse it. The alleged offending parties may also request access to the non-confidential version of the file at any stage during the investigation procedure.[19]

Once the evidence-gathering process has been concluded, the Executive Directorate will submit a copy of the file with all the evidence to the investigated parties. They may present their objections and further evidence within 10 working days. Within 30 working days from the receipt of the investigated parties' submissions, the Executive Directorate will either present an investigation report to the Board of Directors or adopt a dismissal decision if it considers that the evidence is not enough to prove an anti-competitive conduct or when it concludes that the investigated conduct does not restrict competition.

The investigation report submitted to the Board of Directors must contain: (i) the observed conduct; (ii) the evidence showing the conduct, (iii) the parties involved; (iv) the effects of the conduct on the market(s); (v) the type of infringement; and (vi) the liability of the investigated parties.

Although as a general rule all documents and information within an investigation are public, the Competition Act provides for the protection of confidential information. In fact, Pro-Competencia, ex officio or at the request of an interested party, can classify any document or information as confidential.[20] However, only commercial sensitive information seems to subject to confidentiality. Protection of confidential information from third parties (e.g., the identity of the complainant) is essential to ensure an effective detection of anti-competitive infringements.

Figure 2.2. Investigation phase

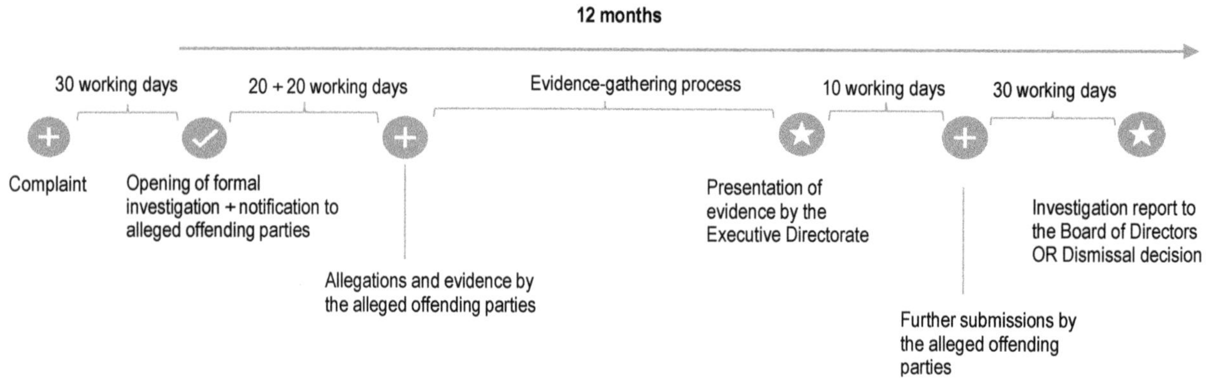

Source: OECD based on information from the Competition Act.

2.3.2. Decision-making phase

The Board of Directors will decide on the admissibility of the case within 30 working days from the receipt of the Executive Directorate's investigation report. The admissibility criteria include: (i) whether the Executive Directorate has met the deadline for presenting the investigation report; (ii) identification of the parties; (iii) the precise charges; (iv) compliance by the Executive Directorate with the legality principle (assess whether the actions of the investigation body have been carried out within the framework of its powers); (v) compliance with due process and rights of defence; and (vi) reasoning of the investigation report. If the case is admitted, the Board of Directors will notify its decision to the alleged offending parties.

Once the case has been admitted, the decision-making takes place in two phases: the evidence phase and the decision phase.

During the evidence phase, the Board of Directors, ex officio or upon request of the parties, holds a public hearing for the submission of further evidence within 15 working days from the notification of admissibility of the case. The purpose of the hearing is to assess new evidence and decide on its admissibility. The parties may appeal for reconsideration against the Board of Director's decision regarding the admission of new evidence within 10 working days.

During the decision phase, the Board of Directors will arrange an additional public hearing to hear the arguments and allegations of the different parties. During this public hearing, the Executive Directorate, the complainant, the witnesses, and the alleged offending parties will be heard. The Board of Director can ask questions and request clarifications to all parties. Once the public hearing has been concluded, the Board of Directors will produce its minutes and may grant an additional reasonable deadline for the alleged offending parties to submit further defence arguments. Once this deadline is over, the Board of Directors has 45 working days to render a final administrative decision on the case.

2.3.3. *Statute of limitation and investigation deadlines*

Investigations are normally subject to a statute of limitation, which refers to a period of limitation to bring actions against certain anti-competitive practice (e.g., a maximum number of years to open an investigation after the alleged illegal practice has ended). In certain countries, investigations also have formal deadlines to be finalised, which sets a maximum period for conducting an investigation (e.g., a maximum number of years to conclude an investigation counting from the opening of the formal proceedings until the adoption of an opinion to the adjudicative body).

In the Dominican Republic, the deadlines for both the statute of limitation and for investigation deadlines are established in the Competition Act.[21]

The statute of limitation is of one year and it starts running from the termination of the alleged unlawful conduct.[22] This is very short compared to statutes of limitations applied in other jurisdictions, as indicated below.

Box 2.4. Statute of limitation periods for competition law infringements

Brazil

In Brazil, the general statute of limitation of anti-competitive infringements is 5 years (and 12 years for cartels) counting from the date of the wrongdoing. For permanent or continuous infringements, the period should be counted from the day that the violation ceased.

Costa Rica

In Costa Rica, the statute of limitation is 4 years, which starts running from the moment the competition authority has knowledge of the conduct or when it had negative effects on competition. For continuous practices, the statute of limitation starts running from the moment of the last fact related to the conduct.

Mexico

In Mexico, the statute of limitation for prosecuting anti-competitive practices is 10 years and starts running from the ceasing of the alleged illegal conduct.

Source: Brazil, Law No. 12 529/2011; Costa Rica, *Ley de Promoción de la Competencia y Defensa Efectiva del Consumidor No. 7472*, 1994 and *Ley de Fortalecimiento de las Autoridades de Competencia de Costa Rica No. 9736*, 2019; Mexico, *Ley Federal de Competencia Económica*, 2014.

Indeed, a short statute of limitation undermines the effectiveness of the competition enforcement, as well as the competition policy more broadly, particularly when related to secret conspiracies such as cartels that are by nature difficult to detect.

The Dominican Competition Act also establishes investigation deadlines, which exists in certain countries, but remains uncommon when it is not followed by proper suspensory mechanisms of the deadlines (e.g., when an information request is sent by the competition authority). In the Dominican Republic, this deadline is 12 months, meaning that the right to prosecute (and thus to sanction) expires if the Executive Directorate takes longer than 12 months to conclude the investigation.[23] The 12-month period can only be suspended under two circumstances:[24]

i) when the parties have objected to the participation of the Executive Director or a member of the Board of Directors for the reasons established in the Criminal Procedural Code (e.g., alleged criminal conviction or negligence in the performance of their duties); or

ii) when the alleged offending parties refuse to reply to a request from the Executive Directorate, provided that all judicial procedures have been exhausted.

The 12-month expiration deadline is too short for carrying out a fully-fledged investigation, collect the necessary evidence and carry out a careful analysis, especially for complex cases. Most jurisdictions do not establish deadlines for conducting investigations. As shown below, jurisdictions with investigation deadlines have opted for longer time limits than those applicable in the Dominican Republic. They also grant the competition authorities with greater flexibility to suspend or extend the investigation period.

Box 2.5. Competition investigation deadlines in Costa Rica, Mexico and Spain

Costa Rica

In Costa Rica, administrative proceedings against competition infringements are divided into two investigation phases: the preliminary phase and the assessment phase. The preliminary phase lasts 12 months and aims at determining whether there is a competition issue and whether there are reasons for opening a formal investigation. The competition authority can extend the preliminary phase for up to six months in certain situations (e.g., if the investigation involves more than one anti-competitive conduct). If the competition authority decides to open a formal investigation, the assessment phase starts and the authority has 10 months to render a decision, which can be extended once for additional six months (e.g., if more time is necessary to analyse new evidence or new facts). Finally, once the assessment phase is over, the competition authority still has 7 months to present its final decision, which can be extended in 1 month only.

Mexico

In Mexico, competition investigations must be carried out within 120 working days, renewable four times, totalling a maximum of 600 working days (around two and half years). The investigation concludes by either submitting a proposal of decision to the Board (the decision-making body) or recommending the closure of the case.

Spain

In Spain, the CNMC has 18 months to complete an administrative proceeding counting from the opening of the investigation to the adoption of the final decision. The investigation phase may only last 12 months, which can be suspend for the following reasons (i) the need to clarify doubts about the evidence or to gather documents from the parties; (ii) a request for information addressed to another public agent; (iii) co-operation process with other jurisdictions; (iv) ongoing administrative appeal (for example, against the inspection decision); (v) the need to produce complementary evidence; and (vi) negotiation of commitments with the investigated parties.

Source: Mexico, *Ley Federal de Competencia Económica*, 2014; Spain, *Ley Defensa de la Competencia No. 15*, 2007 and *Real Decreto No. 261 Reglamento de Defensa de la Competencia*, 2008; Costa Rica, *Ley de Promoción de la Competencia y Defensa Efectiva del Consumidor No. 7472*, 1994 and *Ley de Fortalecimiento de las Autoridades de Competencia de Costa Rica No. 9736*, 2019.

2.4. Enforcement powers

The Competition Act and the Implementing Regulation establish the powers of Pro-Competencia to investigate and sanction anti-competitive conducts. Investigation and detection tools include *ex officio* investigations, dawn raids, requests for information, and statements during interrogations.

2.4.1. Detection tools

According to Article 36 of the Competition Act, the Executive Directorate may start investigations *ex officio* (if it suspects that a behaviour breaches the law) or following a complaint by a party with a legitimate interest.

Complaints must be submitted in writing. They must contain the following elements: (i) the name and contact details of the complainant; (ii) the name and contact details of the alleged infringers; (iii) the facts and evidence regarding the alleged infringement; (iv) if the complainant requests interim measures, the measures envisaged and the risks for the market and the complainant derived from not adopting them; and (v) confidentiality request for sensitive information contained in the complaint.[25]

Complainants must also prove the legitimate interest by submitting evidence that the alleged infringement is causing or may cause them substantial economic damage.[26] Infringements may be reported remotely, using an electronic complaint filing system available at Pro-Competencia's website (Pro-Competencia, 2020[9]), but it is not possible to submit an anonymous competition complaint in the Dominican Republic.

The Executive Directorate must decide on the validity of complaints within 30 working days. Decisions admitting or rejecting complaints must be reasoned and based on a preliminary investigation. Complaints will be considered valid if they contain the above-mentioned elements and include documentary evidence of the alleged facts.

If the complaint is admitted, the Executive Directorate will issue a decision to open a formal investigation and notify it to the parties. The Competition Act provides for inconsistent deadlines for the notification of the opening of a formal investigation. Article 39 of the Competition Act provides for a 3 working-day deadline from the acceptance of the complaint, while Article 44 for a 5 working-day deadline. Together with the notification of the opening of a formal investigation, the parties will receive the complaint, a description of the facts and all supporting evidence submitted by the complainant.

The Executive Directorate must publish on Pro-Competencia's website all admitted complaints and ex-officio investigations. Parties with legitimate interests may submit information or request to intervene as third parties in the procedure within 10 working days after the publication.[27]

When it comes to anti-competitive infringements (and cartels in particular), detection methods can be pro-active or reactive. While pro-active methods are started by the competition authority and do not depend on an external event, reactive methods rely on an external event to occur before the competition authority becomes aware of an issue (Hüschelrath, 2010[10]). Complaints (by competitors, customers, other agencies or current or former employees), external information (e.g., whistle-blowers and informants), and leniency application are examples of reactive methods. Examples of pro-active methods include the use of economics (e.g., collusion factors, industry studies and market screening), use of information from past cases (including from other jurisdictions), industry monitoring (e.g., press and internet, career tracking of industry managers and regular contact with industry representatives), co-operation between agencies (national or foreign competition authorities or other agencies) and technology-led screens (e.g., structural screens and behavioural screens) (OECD, 2023[11]).

Although Pro-Competencia has the power to initiate ex-officio investigations, these are still incipient.[28] As already mentioned, the Dominican competition authority has very limited resources, both as regards material (e.g., technological devices) and human, and therefore the use of reactive detection methods is limited.[29]

The OECD Recommendation concerning Effective Action against Hard Core Cartels recognises the importance of ex officio investigations, stating that jurisdictions should use pro-active cartel detection tools, such as analysis of public procurement data, to trigger and support cartel investigations (OECD, 2019[12]). Indeed, there has been a rise in the interest of competition authorities to use screens to detect cartels worldwide, considering the increasing availability of large amounts of digital data on prices and quantities, as well as the emergence of new technologies to extract and analyse data in an increasingly automated manner (OECD, 2022[13]).

As for reactive detection methods, complaints have played a major role in the Dominican Republic. Since 2017, Pro-Competencia has received 59 complaints: 27 related to unfair competition practices, 9 to cartel offences, 5 to abuse of dominance (and the rest to other types of infringements).

However, the fact that it is not possible to submit an anonymous complaint may prevent those aware of an infringement to report it for fear of retaliation (e.g., firing or blacklisting from the industry). Accordingly, the Recommendation concerning Effective Action against Hard Core Cartels encourages jurisdictions to facilitate the reporting of information on cartels by whistle-blowers, providing appropriate safeguards protecting the anonymity of the informants (OECD, 2019[12]).

Moreover, the requirement to publish complaints and the full version of the decisions to open formal investigations may be detrimental to the next steps of the investigation procedure (either ex officio or initiated after a complaint), particularly in cartels cases as it may contain confidential or sensitive information for the investigation.

Finally, the Dominican Republic does not enjoy a leniency policy to fight cartels, which has often been a powerful detection tool in many jurisdictions including some in Latin America, although the number of leniency applications have dropped worldwide (OECD, 2023[11]).

One of the most important objectives for introducing a leniency program is detection. As perpetrators are generally aware of the illegality of their behaviour, they make significant efforts to conceal their activities. At least in theory, a leniency policy increases the probability of detection and effective punishment of secret conspiracies such as cartels and white-collar crimes in general. It can also help to uncover cartels that would otherwise go undetected and destabilises existing cartels. Another objective for setting up a leniency regime is deterrence. When thinking about taking part in a cartel, companies will consider the likelihood of being detected and sanctioned. A functioning leniency programme is likely to increase the possibility of cartel activity to be uncovered because it raises uncertainty as whether other cartel members will use the tool to denounce the anti-competitive agreement (OECD, 2018[14]).

Nevertheless, two of the prerequisites for an effective leniency programme to work is a high risk of detection and significant sanctions. Leniency will generally work well if the relevant competition authority has built up a sufficient level of credibility as to its capacity to detect and punish cartel infringements and if cartel members perceive a genuine risk that competition authorities might detect and establish a cartel infringement, even without recourse to a leniency programme. A functioning leniency programme also depends on whether the sanctions for those cartel members (both individuals and companies) that do not qualify for leniency are significant. Ideally, fines should outweigh the potential cartel yields so that they cannot simply be regarded as a "profitable" activity. Within the last 20 years, there has been a worldwide trend to increase fines against companies as well as against individuals (OECD, 2017[15]).

Pro-Comptencia has adopted an internal mechanism to reduce fines in exchange of collaboration,[30] which has some similarities with leniency policies as it increases the quality of evidence and makes stronger cases, although not properly a detection tool. This will be examined further in Section 2.4.5.

2.4.2. Dawn raids

Since 2017, Pro-Competencia has only carried out two dawn raids: one related to the cartel sanctioned in the pharmaceutical market (see Box 2.2) and the other related to an ongoing investigation involving public procurement of medicinal oxygen.

The Competition Act allows Pro-Competencia to carry out two types of inspections: (i) announced inspections with the authorisation of the investigated company; or (ii) unannounced inspections (dawn raids) with a search warrant issued by a competent court, which has been the preferred option since it is often more effective for the investigations. Indeed, the previous request for an announced inspection increases the risk of relevant pieces of evidence being destroyed, which otherwise could have helped the prosecution of wrongdoings.

In terms of procedure, the Competition Act requires that authorisations for unannounced inspections are requested in accordance with the Criminal Procedural Code before a criminal court. This seems inconsistent with the powers granted to Pro-Competencia to conduct inspections in relation to administrative infringements and may increase the standard of proof needed for judges to grant the authorisations for administrative dawn raids. Indeed, in the two successful cases mentioned above it was necessary to build a link between the alleged cartel and a suspicious of money laundering and IP criminal offences to seek judicial authorisation for the dawn raids. In practice, the context and the facts of the individual cases may not always allow this kind of adjustments, which can be detrimental for future cartel investigations.

Additional obstacles relate to internal preliminary steps required by the Competition Act for the use of dawn raids: the Executive Directorate, in charge of the investigations in Pro-Competencia, should first request authorisation to the Board of Directors, who according to the Competition Act is the body entitled to access the premises of the undertakings (although this does not happen in practice) and to request the search warrant before the competent judge with the assistance of the Attorney General's Office.[31] A greater separation between investigative and adjudicative powers would seem more aligned to common international practices given the dual system in place in the Dominican Republic, which provides an investigation body (Executive Directorate) and an adjudication body (Board of Directors) within Pro-Competencia.

To safeguard the constitutional rights of defence, Pro-Competencia carries out dawn raids once the alleged offending parties have been notified of the initiation of a formal investigation,[32] although this is likely to undermine the surprise effect, which is a key feature of the unannounced inspections. In any case, in practice, the Executive Directorate notifies the investigated parties of the initiation of the formal investigation just before submitting the court order authorising the dawn raid and just before entering the premises.

Once the dawn raid is in course, the Executive Directorate may search the premises, the properties, and the means of transport of economic agents to gather evidence, with the support of the National Police (*Dirección de la Policía Nacional*, DPN). The Executive Directorate may also make extracts and copies of books, documents, and accounting records of the investigated parties, which can be collected on paper or electronically.[33] In practice, most incriminating evidence in competition cases is found in electronic form, and IT forensic equipment allows gathering electronic evidence in a safe manner, ensuring the source of information and the chain of custody. As Pro-competencia does not have IT forensic equipment, it gathers digital evidence with the help of and using the IT forensic tools of the National Police. While collaboration with National Police is positive, competition authorities should also be able to develop their own IT forensic expertise, including the necessary staff and equipment, to increase autonomy in cartel investigations.

The Competition Act also imposes an obligation of co-operation to inspected parties during inspections and sanctions and/or the use of state force can be used to ensure the effectiveness of the general provision of obligation to co-operate. Although the Competition Act establishes the possibility of sanction in case of non-compliance of this obligation, it re-directs to Article 64 that does not contain any information on sanctions.[34]

2.4.3. Requests for information

The Competition Act and the Implementing Regulation[35] establishes that Pro-Competencia may request firms to provide information, data or documents at any time during the administrative procedure. Information requests can be sent to investigated parties, but also to third parties. Both investigated and third parties are formally obliged by law to reply to request for information,[36] although the Competition Act does not provide any fines for absence of a response or a delay in replying. Indeed, only the submission of false information may be subject to fines imposed by Pro-Competencia.[37] However, Article 58 of the Competition Act states that those that do not comply with the requests of Pro-Competencia's Board of Directors will be subject to the criminal sanctions provided in the Dominican Criminal Code. Such infringements should be prosecuted by the public prosecutor's office.

According to the OECD Recommendation concerning Effective Action against Hard Core Cartels, competition authorities must have effective powers to investigate hard core cartels, including the powers to request and obtain information from investigated and third parties, and also to impose sanctions for non-compliance with mandatory requests and obstruction of investigations (OECD, 2019[12]). The same is also relevant for abuse of dominance cases.

In addition, requests for information do not suspend the 12-months period that Pro-Competencia has to complete its investigation, which also negatively affects the effectivity of this enforcement tool in antitrust investigations. More information about the investigation time-limits including statutes of limitation were examined further above in Section 2.3.3.

The Executive Directorate may also interview and record statements from defendants. The Competition Act provides that interviews to investigated parties must be done in the presence of their defence attorney. The minutes of the interview must be signed by the interviewed party or his/her refusal to sign recorded in writing. The Competition Act is silent regarding the procedural rights applicable to interviews conducted to third parties, and the Executive Directorate applies in practice the procedural guarantees observed in the law for investigated parties when recording statements from other parties.

As for the requests for information made to other government entities by Pro-Competencia, these are mainly governed by the collaboration principle enshrined in Article 12 of the Organic Law of Public Administration (*Ley Órganica de la Administración* Pública, LOAP) and not properly by the Competition Act.

2.4.4. Interim measures

The Competition Act provides that Pro-Competencia can issue interim measures before the adoption of a final administrative decision to ensure the effectiveness of its enforcement powers. Article 64 establishes the general criteria for granting interim measures: (i) to ensure the effectiveness of an eventual sanctioning decision; (ii) if there is no possibility of causing irreparable harm to the parties that will be affected by such measures; and (iii) when their adoption is in accordance with the law. The interim measures are limited to the ceasing of the alleged infringing conduct and the establishment of a guarantee to cover the damages that the interim measures may cause.[38]

Nevertheless, the Competition Act is not clear regarding who is the competent authority within Pro-Competencia to grant interim measures. The understanding of Pro-Competencia is that the Executive Directorate has such power, and the Board of Directors can review interim measures imposed by the Executive Directorate.[39] The first interim measure granted by the Executive Directorate was issued in April 2023.[40]

In addition, Pro-Competencia, through the Board of Directors, can request the competent court to issue interim measures.[41] Interim measures granted by courts are not limited to refrain from acting (negative injunction), and could therefore include a positive injunction (i.e., requiring the parties to act). Although interim measures are usually more useful during the investigation phase, neither the law nor the Implementing Regulation explain the role of the Executive Directorate in the requests for interim measures before courts. In practice, the Board of Directors has requested interim measures before judicial courts with the support of the Executive Directorate. Since 2017, Pro-Competencia has requested interim measures in relation to six cases, but the Judiciary has not granted any of its requests. These procedures lasted from 3 to 7 months, which seem long given that interim measures usually serve to protect imminent and irreparable harm, amongst other requirements that will be examined below.[42]

According to international practices, interim measures are granted by public authorities or courts with a protective and corrective objective, i.e., providing temporary relief pending the outcome of a case. In addition, interim measures are commonly granted in exceptional circumstances, and they typically require meeting two key conditions: the likelihood of success on the merits of the case and the urgency to prevent harm (OECD, 2022[16]).

The adoption of interim measures is a powerful and intrusive tool. It requires indeed a balancing exercise between an expedited procedure to urgently (and effectively) act to prevent serious and irreparable harm and the rights of defence of the parties involved. Many jurisdictions have put in place interim measures procedures with essential safeguards to preserve such rights. According to the Implementing Regulation, the Board of Directors must establish the administrative procedure for the adoption of interim measures, but this has not yet been established.[43]

2.4.5. Sanctions, settlements and commitments

In the Dominican Republic, both undertakings and individuals (e.g., legal representatives or directors of an undertaking)[44] can be sanctioned for anti-competitive infringements. Article 61 of the Competition Act establishes the following sanctions:

a) Fines from 200 to 3 000 monthly minimum wages for bid rigging offences.

b) Fines from 30 to 3 000 monthly minimum wage for concerted practices and agreements consisting of price fixing, market allocation, output limitation, elimination of competitors or impeding access to market and abuses of dominant position.

c) Fines from 50 to 200 monthly minimum wages for providing false information to Pro-Competencia.

The Competition Act sets the fines based on minimum wages, which differ across economic sectors in the Dominican Republic, and thus are calculated on the basis of the minimum wage applicable to the sector where the anti-competitive conduct took place.[45] According to the Labour Ministry (*Ministerio de Trabajo*), the average minimum wage in the country was DOP 17 873 (around EUR 300) in January 2023 (Presidencia de la República Dominicana, 2023[17]). In practice, this means that fines are between EUR 9 000 and EUR 900 000, which seem very low particularly for certain markets that have great profits and turnovers.

Although the Competition Act establishes a fine for providing false information to Pro-Competencia, it does not contain any sanction for failure to reply, late replies nor for the use of incomplete or misleading information, which are common in other jurisdictions and necessary to ensure that the effectiveness of the investigative powers of the competition authority.

The table below compares the maximum level of competition fines for undertakings in some jurisdictions in the region. Such jurisdictions provide for maximum levels of fines based on a percentage of turnover or a combination of the latter with a specific monetary amount. This allows for more proportionality and flexibility when applying sanctions, enabling competition authorities to better consider the size of the company and the impact of the conduct on the market.

Table 2.1. Maximum level of competition fines for undertakings in selected jurisdictions in Latin America

Jurisdiction	Legislation	Maximum penalty
Brazil	Art. 37 of Law No. 12 529/2011	20% of the revenue of the economic group investigated in the economic sector in which happened the illegal conduct. If it is possible to estimate the economic advantage obtained with the anti-competitive conduct, the fine must not be inferior to that.
Chile	Art. 26 of Decree-Law No. 211 from 1973 (updated in 2016)	If it is possible to determine the line of products or services related to the illegal practice or the economic advantage obtained with the conduct investigated, the penalties can be alternatively: 30% of the amount sold of the products or services; or double of the economic advantage.
Colombia	Art. 4, item 15 of Decree No. 2153/1992 (modified by Law No. 1340/2009)	Up to 100 thousand times the "Tax Unit Value" (UVT), equivalent to approximately COP 4 billion (around EUR 900 000) or 150% of the economic advantage, if it is possible to obtain.
Costa Rica	Art. 119 of Law No. 9736/2019	10% of the total revenue of the investigated company in the previous fiscal year of the penalty imposition.
Ecuador	Art. 79 of Law of Regulation and Control of Market Power from 2011	12% of the total gross revenue of the company or economic group in the previous year of the penalty imposition.
Mexico	Art. 127 of Federal Law of Economic Competition from 2014	10% of the total revenue of the company within the country in the previous fiscal year of the illegal conduct.

Source: OECD based on public information.

Proportionate fines are critical to deter companies from breaching the law, which should not be perceived as a profitable activity. Ideally, fines should outweigh the potential returns of infringements divided by the probability of detection (Ginsburg and Wright, 2010[18]; Connor and Lande, 2012[19]). If the expected infringement gains are higher than the expected fine, rational companies might neither consider applying for leniency nor abstain from engaging in anti-competitive conduct (OECD, 2019[20]).

To determine the exact amount of a fine, the following criteria should be taken into consideration by Pro-Competencia:[46]

a) scope and type of the competition restriction;
b) the size of the affected markets;
c) the anti-competitive effects on actual or potential competitors, consumers and users;
d) premeditation and intent;
e) market share of the infringer;
f) duration of the infringement; and
g) recidivism and offender's criminal and infringement record.

In case of recidivism, an additional fine of up to the double of the fine may be imposed. Moreover, in case the infringer refuses to pay, the amount of the fine may be increased by 3% percent each month until the infringer pays the due amount.

In 2017, the Board of Directors adopted a Decision[47] explaining how the competition authority calculates one of the elements necessary to estimate the fine, i.e., the damage caused by the anti-competitive practice (see Box 2.6).

Box 2.6. Methodologies to calculate the damage caused by competition law infringements

In its Decision No. 021-2017, Pro-Competencia indicates that the quantification of the damages caused by an anti-competitive conduct is mainly based on determining what would have happened if the economic agents did not engage in anti-competitive behaviour. This scenario is commonly known as the counterfactual. Since the counterfactual cannot be directly observed, it is necessary to build it. The decision provides for different methodologies to estimate the counterfactual, namely:

- Historical comparison in the market, comparing the situation during the period in which the infringement takes place with the situation in the market before the infringement, or after the effects of the anti-competitive conduct have ceased.
- Comparison with other geographic markets and product markets where the infringement did not take place.
- Difference-in-difference method, which compares the evolution of the economic variable under study (for example, price) in the market affected by the infringement during a given period of time with the evolution of the same variable during the same period in an unaffected market.

Once the counterfactual has been determined, the decision proposes to use different methods to estimate the economic variable that would be used to calculate the damage, for instance: average, median, linear interpolation, regression analysis, simulation models, methods based on costs and financial analysis.

Additionally, the decision recommends analysing other unrelated elements to establish to what extent the damage could be explained by factors other than by the competition law infringement. Elements not related to the conduct and that could be relevant for conducting this assessment include market regulation, costs of inputs and external market shocks, such as inflation.

Source: Pro-Competencia (2017[21]), Decision No. 021-2017, https://procompetencia.gob.do/wp-content/uploads/2020/02/res_021-1720que20aprueba20criterios20determinacion20y20cuantificacion20del20dano1.pdf.

Pro-Competencia's initiative to provide clarity in the calculation of damage in competition cases is welcome, but it does not tackle the main issue related to the low fines, particularly the low cap for maximum fines in the country (maximum of around EUR 900 000). This would require a change in the Competition Act.

The obligations created by collusive practices sanctioned by Pro-Competencia are automatically null and void.[48] Pro-Competencia cannot impose non-monetary sanctions (e.g., director disqualification and bidder exclusion), which are common in several jurisdictions and can be a powerful general deterrence mechanism (OECD, 2022[22]).

Settlements are also an important mechanism for enforcement usually used to shorten the investigation procedure (which saves costs for the public administration) and/or reinforce a given investigation with better evidence (e.g., policies related to reduction of fines in exchange of collaboration). Indeed, many competition regimes around the world offer the possibility to early terminate competition investigations, commonly referred to as settlements and commitments (usually the first applied for cartel cases and the second to abuse of dominance cases, e.g. with a commitment to allow access to an essential facility).

The Implementing Regulation provides for an early termination tool that contains features of both settlement and commitment mechanisms,[49] although this tool has never been used in practice: Pro-Competencia has not yet received any request for settlement nor commitment. This scenario can hopefully change with the enactment of two regulations by Pro-Competencia in 2021, providing a framework for mechanisms related to settlements and commitments.[50]

Besides being an administrative infringement to be sanctioned by Pro-Competencia (or the sector regulators with competition enforcement powers), cartel conduct is a criminal offence in the Dominican Republic, and it is punishable by a fine and imprisonment from one month to two years, as per Article 419 of the Dominican Criminal Code. Pro-Competencia has no authority to enforce criminal law, which falls to the Dominican public prosecutors.

Programme of Collaboration and Reduction of Fines

In June 2021, the Board of Directors adopted a Decision[51] to establish a "Programme of Collaboration and Reduction of Fines". It provides for the reduction of sanctions in exchange of collaboration during investigations related to collusive agreements, in particular cartels.

The programme provides a marker system in which firms that apply first get a greater fine reduction than firms that apply later. The first applicant will get a fine equal to the minimum level of fines established in the Competition Act for the corresponding type of infringement, while the second and the subsequent applicants will get a reduction between 50% and 70%. The overall conditions to benefit from the a "Programme of Collaboration and Reduction of Fines" are the following:

a) Acknowledgement of participation in the anti-competitive agreement.
b) Provide evidence that is relevant and conclusive to prove the existence of an anti-competitive agreement.
c) Provide evidence that adds value to the investigation procedure, i.e., that the information is new because the Executive Directorate has not had access to it or would never have access to it unless provided by the applicant.
d) Provide the evidence before the closing of the investigation phase.
e) Full, continuous and diligent co-operation during the investigation phase.
f) No evidence of the alleged anti-competitive behaviour must have been destroyed, falsified, or concealed.
g) Keep the request confidential until the Board of Directors issues a decision putting an end to the administrative procedure.
h) Stop the anti-competitive conduct unless otherwise requested by the competition authority.
i) Neither being a repeat offender nor having previously benefited from the programme.
j) Not having forced or threatened other members of the cartel to form part of it.

The Decision also provides the procedural steps and deadlines for submitting and accepting such applications. The programme is sometimes improperly called leniency in the Dominican Republic, although it does not offer immunity to any of the beneficiary firms, and it is not established in the Competition Act.

A firm benefiting from the programme can lose the benefit of fine reduction in the following situations: (i) if it refutes the acknowledged facts; (ii) if it does not comply with the request of the Executive Directorate to verify or to ratify the information provided or the acknowledged facts; and/or (iii) if it destroys, alters or obstructs access to information or evidence.

At the time of writing, this programme has never been used in practice and was being reviewed by Pro-Competencia.

Programme of Cease-and-Desist Commitments

Also in June 2021, Pro-Competencia issued a Decision[52] providing a framework for a programme focused on cease-and-desist commitments in the context of early termination procedures. In a nutshell, it requires that the parties admit liability and commit to cease the conduct under investigation and the following requirements should be met:

1. They must effectively solve in a clear and unequivocal manner the competition issues that led to the initiation of the investigation.
2. The remedies can be implemented timely and effectively.
3. The monitoring of the compliance and the effectiveness of the remedies must be feasible and effective.
4. The likely effects of the alleged anti-competitive conduct have not seriously harmed the market and the consumer welfare. For assessing the likely effects of the alleged conduct, Pro-Competencia will take into consideration, among others, the affected market, the duration of the alleged conduct, the number of companies or consumers presumably affected.

The Decision also provides the procedural steps and deadlines for submitting and accepting such applications.

The investigations can be resumed if, during the one-year monitoring period: (i) there is a material change in any of the facts or data that constituted the essential elements of the decision; (ii) the conditions of a remedy have been breached; or (iii) the early termination decision was based on false information. If Pro-Competencia reinitiates an infringement investigation, the undertakings could be sanctioned in accordance with the rules applicable to recidivists if the same conduct that motivated the adoption of the early termination decision is established. Moreover, an economic operator can request to the Board of Directors a review of its remedies.

At the time of writing, this programme had never been used in practice and was also being reviewed by Pro-Competencia.

2.2. Judicial review

Pro-Competencia's infringement decisions against anti-competitive and unfair competition practices may be reviewed by administrative courts. Parties may appeal against Pro-Competencia's decisions before the Superior Administrative Court (*Tribunal Superior Administrativo*, TSA). During the proceedings before the TSA, the public interest is represented by the Administrative Attorney General and Pro-Competencia acts as a defendant.[53]

Decisions of the Superior Administrative Court may be subject to appeal on points of law (*recurso de casación*) before the Supreme Court of Justice (*Suprema Corte de Justicia*), the highest jurisdictional body in the Dominican Republic.[54]

At the time of writing, the Superior Administrative Court had reviewed the two infringement decisions that Pro-Competencia had adopted: the cartel decision was upheld, while the abuse of dominance decision was annulled. These judgements do not contain discussions regarding substantive competition law matters, but rather focus on procedural aspects. Both judgements have been appealed before the Supreme Court of Justice, and final decisions were still pending.

Dominican judges in charge of reviewing competition infringement decisions have an administrative and constitutional law background and are not specialised in competition law. Some judges received competition law training in 2008, when the Competition Act was formally adopted, but since then judges have not received further capacity building on the topic.

One of the criteria for the promotion of judges in the Dominican Republic is capacity building. The National School for the Judiciary (*Escuela Nacional de la Judicatura*, ENJ) offers specialised training for judges and other officials in the national judiciary system. The ENJ encourages new and innovative learning methodologies and offers in-person and online courses through its virtual platform. During the fact-finding mission, the Judiciary indicated that the ENJ chooses the topics of training based on surveys conducted among the judges, but it would also be open to training proposals from other government entities, such as Pro-Competencia.

Reviewing competition enforcement decisions requires a good understanding of competition law, including its legal concepts and economic principles. Ideally, judges reviewing competition decisions should have experience and expertise in the interpretation of competition law to balance two of their main functions, i.e., ensuring due process and applying, when appropriate, substantive economic principles into their reasoning (OECD, 2016[23]).

According to an ICN survey conducted during 2013-2014 with 49 jurisdictions, the activities that have proven most successful to increase the courts knowledge on technical economic issues are tailor-made capacity building activities, such as conferences, seminars, workshops and training programmes (OECD, 2015[24]).

International organisations may play a key role in providing, supporting and facilitating capacity-building initiatives, such as technical assistance, training programmes, seminars or expert meetings, among others (OECD, 2016[23]). Box 2.7 shows an example of a capacity-building initiative for judges organised by the OECD in the region.

Box 2.7. Capacity-building for judges organised by the OECD Regional Centre for Competition

In July 2022, the OECD Regional Centre for Competition in Latin America organised a Workshop on "Judicial Review of Antitrust Enforcement". The workshop covered the central role that the Judiciary plays in competition policy, particularly in relation to cartel and abuse of dominance cases. It gathered 332 participants from 19 jurisdictions in Latin America and the Caribbean (among which the Dominican Republic) including competition officials and judges.

During the workshop, the following issues were discussed by experts: dawn raids; interim measures; the standard of proof and the use of indirect evidence; judicial review of fines and other sanctions; and the role of economics and economists. Finally, judges and courts shared their country experiences with the audience.

Source: OECD (2022[25]), Annual Report of Activities: Regional Centre for Competition in Latin America, https://www.oecd.org/daf/competition/oecd-rcc-lima-annual-report-2022-en.pdf.

2.3. Private enforcement

Anti-competitive and unfair competition practices may give rise to different types of civil actions. Civil damage claims are possible in relation to both anti-competitive and unfair competition practices. In addition to damage claims, the parties affected by unfair competition practices may bring civil actions to request for injunctive relief.

Regarding anti-competitive conduct cases, Article 63 of the Competition Act provides that only undertakings that have proven, during the administrative proceedings, to have suffered harm from the anti-competitive conduct are able to claim damages. Neither individuals nor undertakings that have not participated in the administrative proceedings or have participated but have not demonstrated any harm from the investigated conduct are, therefore, eligible to claim compensation for damages before a civil judge. As for unfair competition cases, both individuals and legal entities that have suffered damages may bring civil damage claims.

Competition damage actions are governed by civil law and filed based on the principle of extracontractual civil liability (tort liability), established in Articles 1382 et seq. of the Dominican Republic Civil Code (*Código Civil de la República Dominicana*).

The Competition Act does not mention whether a final decision of Pro-Competencia is a condition for bringing a damage action in anti-competitive conduct cases. Thus, in principle both follow-on and stand-alone actions would be possible. However, it is unclear what would be the probatory value of Pro-Competencia's decisions in follow-on actions.

In unfair competition cases that are being investigated by Pro-Competencia, only follow-on actions are possible. As explained in Section 3.2.2, parties affected by unfair competition practices may choose to launch a judicial proceeding by bringing an action before a court or trigger an administrative investigation by lodging a complaint before Pro-Competencia. If the party chooses the latter alternative, it can only claim damages when the matter has been decided by the last judicial instance.

Damage actions regarding unfair competition practices seem to be more developed in the Dominican Republic, while civil actions resulting from anti-competitive conduct are unused. Indeed, no information has been provided on any competition damage claim case.

Main findings

The main findings on competition law enforcement in the Dominican Republic include:

- In the field of merger control, the telecommunications regulator analyses the competition effects of the transactions, while the electricity and financial sectors only focus on regulatory aspects. The rest of the economy is not subject to merger control enforcement.
- Enforcement against anti-competitive practices is incipient. While Pro-Competencia has only sanctioned two competition cases (regarding cartel and abuse of dominance, respectively), sector regulators with competition enforcement powers have only adopted one enforcement decision related to competition law (i.e., in the telecommunications sector). No bid-rigging cases have been sanctioned and only two cases are currently ongoing.
- Concerning sanctions, the maximum fines established by the Competition Act are very low and based on minimum wages, with no deterrent effects on companies.
- There is no leniency policy to fight cartels, although Pro-Competencia has adopted an internal mechanism to reduce fines (but not to grant immunity) in exchange of collaboration, with some similarities with leniency policies. Pro-Competencia has also introduced settlement and commitment mechanisms for an early termination of investigations, but they have never been used in practice.
- Investigations are subject to a statute of limitation of one year that starts from the termination of the alleged anti-competitive practice, which seems very short compared to other jurisdictions.
- Investigations are also subject to a 12-months deadline to be finalised, which seems too short, especially in complex cases. In addition, the 12-month expiration deadline can only be suspended in very limited circumstances.

References

Connor, J. and R. Lande (2012), "Cartel as Rational Business Strategy: Crime Pays", *Cardozo Law Review*, Vol. 34/2, pp. 427-490. [19]

Ginsburg, D. and J. Wright (2010), "Antitrust Sanctions", *Competition Policy International*, Vol. 6/2, pp. 3-39. [18]

Hüschelrath, K. (2010), *How Are Cartels Detected? The Increasing Use of Proactive Methods to Establish Antitrust Infringements*, pp. 522-528. [10]

INDOTEL (2017), *Decision No. 056-17*, https://transparencia.indotel.gob.do/wp-content/uploads/2022/10/res-no-056-17.pdf. [5]

INDOTEL (2017), *Decision No. 077-17*, https://transparencia.indotel.gob.do/wp-content/uploads/2022/10/res-077-17-fusion-altice-recurso-de-reconsideracion-contra-la-056-17.pdf. [6]

OECD (2023), *Competition and Sports, Latin American and Carribbean Competition Forum, Background Note by the Secretariat*, https://one.oecd.org/document/DAF/COMP/LACCF(2023)5/en/pdf. [11]

OECD (2023), *OECD Services Trade Restrictiveness Index: Policy trends up to 2023*, OECD Publishing, https://www.oecd.org/trade/topics/services-trade/. [2]

OECD (2022), *Data Screening Tools in Competition Investigations, OECD Competition Policy Roundtable Background Note*, https://www.oecd.org/daf/competition/data-screening-tools-in-competition-investigations-2022.pdf. [13]

OECD (2022), *Director Disqualification and Bidder Exclusion in Competition Enforcement, OECD Competition Policy Roundtable Background Note*, https://www.oecd.org/daf/competition/director-disqualification-and-bidder-exclusion-in-competition-enforcement-2022.pdf. [22]

OECD (2022), *Media Mergers, Latin American and Carribbean Competition Forum, Note by the Secretariat*, https://one.oecd.org/document/DAF/COMP/LACF(2022)18/en/pdf. [16]

OECD (2022), *Multi-dimensional Review of the Dominican Republic: Towards Greater Well-being for All, OECD Development Pathways*, OECD Publishing, https://doi.org/10.1787/560c12bf-en. [25]

OECD (2021), *Global Merger Control: OECD Competition Trends, Volume II, OECD Publishing*, http://www.oecd.org/competition/oecd-competition-trends.htm. [1]

OECD (2020), *OECD Peer Reviews of Competition Law and Policy: Mexico*, https://www.oecd.org/daf/competition/Mexico-Peer-Reviews-of-Competition-Law-and-Policy-en.pdf. [26]

OECD (2019), *Competition in Labour Markets, OECD Competition Policy Roundtable Background Note*, https://www.oecd.org/daf/competition/competition-concerns-in-labour-markets.htm. [20]

OECD (2019), *Recommendation of the Council concerning Effective Action against Hard Core Cartels*, https://legalinstruments.oecd.org/en/instruments/OECD-LEGAL-0452. [12]

OECD (2018), *OECD Review of the Corporate Governance of State-Owned Enterprises: Argentina*, https://www.oecd.org/daf/ca/Argentina-SOE-Review.pdf. [14]

OECD (2017), *The Implementation of the Council Recommendation concerning Effective Action against Hard Core Cartels*, OECD Publishing, https://one.oecd.org/document/DAF/COMP/WP3(2017)2/en/pdf. [15]

OECD (2016), *The resolution of competition cases by specialised and generalist courts: Stocktaking of international experiences*, OECD Publishing, https://www.oecd.org/daf/competition/The-resolution-of-competition-cases-by-Specialised-and-Generalist-Courts. [23]

OECD (2015), *Summary Record: Annex to the Summary Record of the 123rd Meeting of the Competition Committee held on 15-19 June 2015. Key points of the Roundtables on Changes in Institutional Design*, OECD Publishing, https://one.oecd.org/document/DAF/COMP/M. [24]

OECD (2005), *Recommendation of the Council on Merger Review*, https://legalinstruments.oecd.org/en/instruments/OECD-LEGAL-0333. [4]

OECD-IDB (2020), *OECD-IDB Peer Reviews of Competition Law and Policy: El Salvador*, https://www.oecd.org/daf/competition/El-Salvador-Peer-Reviews-of-Competition-Law-and-Policy-2020.pdf. [27]

OECD-IDB (2018), *OECD-IDB Peer Review of Competition Law and Policy in Peru*, https://www.oecd.org/daf/competition/PERU-Peer-Reviews-of-Competition-Law-and-Policy-2018.pdf. [3]

Presidencia de la República Dominicana (2023), *Ministerio de Trabajo aclara salario mínimo es mayor que en seis países de Latinoamérica*, https://presidencia.gob.do/noticias/ministerio-de-trabajo-aclara-salario-minimo-es-mayor-que-en-seis-paises-de-latinoa. [17]

Pro-Competencia (2021), *Decisión n. 010-2021*, https://procompetencia.gob.do/wp-content/uploads/2021/06/resolucion-num-010-2021-version-publica.pdf. [7]

Pro-Competencia (2021), *Decision No. 008-2021*, https://procompetencia.gob.do/wp-content/uploads/2021/06/cd-008-2021-que-aprueba-rrs-por-colaboracioin.pdf. [28]

Pro-Competencia (2021), *Decision No. 011-2021: Reglamento para el Sometimiento y Aprobación de Compromisos de Cese en el Marco de las Investigaciones por Violacion a la Ley General de Defensa de la Competencia*, https://procompetencia.gob.do/wp-content/uploads/2021/07/cd-011-2021-reglamento-compromiso-de-cese.pdf. [30]

Pro-Competencia (2020), *Recepción y tramitación de denuncias*, https://procompetencia.gob.do/servicios/recepcion-y-tramitacion-de-denuncias/. [9]

Pro-Competencia (2018), *Decision 018-2018*, https://procompetencia.gob.do/resoluciones-procompetencia/resolucion-num-018-2018. [8]

Pro-Competencia (2017), *Decision 021-2017*, https://procompetencia.gob.do/wp-content/uploads/2020/02/res_021-1720que20aprueba20criterios20determinacion20y20cuantificacion20del20dano1.pdf. [21]

Pro-Competencia (2017), *Decision No. 021-2017*, https://procompetencia.gob.do/wp-content/uploads/2020/02/res_021-1720que20aprueba20criterios20determinacion20y20cuantificacion20del20dano1.pdf. [29]

Notes

[1] Article 12 of Regulation of fair and free competition for the public telecommunication services, adopted by Decision No. 022-05, https://www.indotel.gob.do/wp-content/uploads/2022/10/36-resolucion-no-022-05-actualizada-con-derogaciones-modf-078-19.pdf.

[2] Ibid.

[3] Article 14 of Regulation of fair and free competition for the public telecommunication services, adopted by Decision No. 022-05.

[4] Article 14.2 of the Regulation of fair and free competition for the public telecommunication services, adopted by No. Decision 022-05.

[5] Ley General de Electricidad No. 125-01, https://www.sie.gob.do/images/sie-documentos-pdf/leyes/LeyGeneraldeElecctricidadNo.125-01.pdf.

[6] Reglamento para la aplicación de la Ley General de Electricidad No. 125-01 aprobado por Decreto No. 555-02, https://www.cne.gob.do/wp-content/uploads/2015/05/Reglamento.Ley_.No_.125-01.pdf.

[7] Article 11 of the LGE and Article 10 of the Implementing Electricity Regulation.

[8] Ibid.

[9] Decision SIE No. 60-2003 from 5 September 2003.

[10] Article 35 of Law No. 183-02 of Dominican Republic that establishes the regulatory framework of monetary and financial system (the "Monetary and Financial Law").

[11] Decision No. 010-2021, from 14 June 2021 (Pro-Competencia, 2021, pp. 99-100[7]).

[12] Article 7, paragraph I of the Competition Act.

[13] Decision No. 010-2021, from 14 June 2021 (Pro-Competencia, 2021, pp. 99-100[7]).

[14] This is the case of Mexico and El Salvador, for example (OECD, 2020[26]) (OECD-IDB, 2020[27])

[15] Article 7, item 2 of the Competition Act.

[16] For example, this is the case in Mexico and El Salvador (OECD, 2020[26]) (OECD-IDB, 2020[27]).

[17] Article 9 of the Competition Act.

[18] Article 39 of the Competition Act.

[19] According to Article 27 of the Implementing Regulation, confidential information includes commercially or industrially valuable sensitive information.

[20] Article 41 of the Competition Act and Article 25 of the Implementing Regulation.

[21] Articles 56 and 57 of the Competition Act.

[22] Article 56 of the Competition Act.

[23] Article 57 of the Competition Act.

[24] Article 38 of the Implementing Regulation.

[25] Article 19 of the Implementing Regulation.

[26] Article 37 of the Competition Act.

[27] Article 40 of the Competition Act.

[28] So far, Pro-Competencia has opened 8 ex-officio investigations against anti-competitive practices, including the two cases that have resulted in sanctions. In addition, Pro-Competencia has initiated one ex-officio investigation against the submission of false information, which also amounted to a sanction.

[29] At the time of writing, Pro-Competencia was developing guidelines on cartel screening techniques, which are likely to help the authority to further engage in ex-officio investigations.

[30] I.e., Decision No. 008-2021 establishing a "Programme of Collaboration and Reduction of Fines" (Pro-Competencia, 2021[28])

[31] Article 31 of the Competition Act.

[32] Article 69 of the Dominican Republic and Articles 39 and 42 of the Competition Act.

[33] Article 42 of the Competition Act.

[34] Articles 42 and 64 of the Competition Act.

[35] Article 42 of the Competition Act and Article 34 of the Implementing Regulation.

[36] Article 40 of the Implementing Regulation.

[37] Article 61, item "d" of the Competition Act.

[38] Article 64 of the Competition Act.

[39] Article 31, item "g" of the Competition Act.

[40] Decision No. DE-004-2023 from 5 April 2023, https://procompetencia.gob.do/wp-content/uploads/2023/04/de-004-2023-firmada-y-sellada-vp.pdf. The investigated party has appealed to the Superior Administrative Court, which at the time of writing had not yet issued a decision.

[41] Article 31, item "f" of the Competition Act.

[42] It should be noted that Article 33, item "f" of the Competition Act establishes that requests for interim measures shall be decided by the competent court within 48 hours.

[43] Article 36 of the Implementing Regulation.

[44] According to Article 60, paragraph I of the Competition Act, individuals who have participated in anti-competitive practices, either directly, as accomplices or concealers, personally or as an employee, or on behalf of a legal entity, shall be sanctioned in line with the Dominican Criminal Procedural Code. In practice, however, no individuals have ever been sanctioned by Pro-Competencia so far.

[45] Article 61 of the Competition Act.

[46] Article 62 of the Competition Act.

[47] Decision No. 021-2017 (Pro-Competencia, 2017[29]).

[48] Article 61, item V of the Competition Act.

[49] Article 21, para. II of the Implementing Regulation.

[50] Namely, Decision No. 08-2011 and Decision No. 011-2021

[51] Decision No. 008-2021 (Pro-Competencia, 2021[28]).

[52] Decision No. 011-2021 (Pro-Competencia, 2021[30])

[53] Articles 51 to 54 of the Competition Act.

[54] Article 54 of the Competition Act.

3 Competition advocacy and institutional co-operation

This section will examine the promotion of competition in the Dominican Republic by Pro-Competencia, as well as its institutional co-operation with national sector regulators and competition authorities in other jurisdictions.

3.1. Competition advocacy

A strong competition authority and a comprehensive competition law is not sufficient for allowing the economy and consumers to reap the benefits of a competitive environment. Indeed, in addition to effective competition enforcement, a competition culture must be established, not only among businesses, but also among courts, politicians, and government authorities, such as sector regulators. In other words, to work properly competition needs support from the policy environment and adequate framework conditions (OECD, 2013[1]).

Promoting competition is particularly relevant in developing countries, where competition law and policy are usually incipient and public policies and regulations are subject to major reviews. In this context, the role of competition authorities is of paramount importance to ensure that the review of regulations take into account competition principles.

Competition advocacy is a powerful tool to build competition culture. Pro-Competencia's advocacy powers include promoting the adoption of regulations and state support measures that do not unduly restrict competition. In addition, Pro-Competencia can promote competition by raising awareness among other government entities, economic agents and the Dominican population about the importance of free competition.[1]

Pro-Competencia has multiple tools to implement its competition advocacy powers. For instance, it can conduct market studies; issue non-binding recommendation reports and non-binding reasoned opinions; prepare guidelines; and carry out training and outreach activities. As described in Section 1.4.1, the Competition Advocacy and Promotion Unit is in charge of preparing non-binding opinions and reports, organising outreach events and preparing guidelines, while the Economic and Market Studies Unit is responsible for carrying out market studies.

Although Pro-Competencia has adopted several advocacy initiatives between 2017 and 2022, a lack of competition culture is still perceived in the country including business.

3.1.1. Reports and opinions

Pro-Competencia can issue public non-binding recommendation reports in relation to:

a) Legal acts (laws, regulations, orders, standards, decisions and other legal instruments) that distort competition.[2]

b) State measures granting subsidies, aid or incentives to public and private companies that may create barriers to entry or confer unfair competitive advantages.[3]

c) Burdensome administrative procedures that hinder competition among companies and their right of establishment.[4]

Furthermore, Pro-Competencia can adopt public non-binding reasoned opinions in relation to acts adopted by sector regulators aimed at regulating markets or adopting infringement decisions in competition matters.[5]

Pro-Competencia's advocacy actions may be triggered *ex officio*, by a complaint or by the obligation of the sector regulators to notify the competition authority of new regulations or sanctioning decisions. Pro-Competencia monitors on a regular basis the activities of the government and the Parliament. For example, Pro-Competencia has screened the development of new draft laws, regulations, administrative procedures and state support measures and examines their potential effects on competition by applying the Competition Assessment Checklist of the OECD Competition Assessment Toolkit (OECD, 2019[2]).

During the examination and assessment of a legal act, a state support measure or an administrative procedure, Pro-Competencia can request the necessary information to government entities. According to Article 13 of the Implementing Regulation, these entities are required to submit the information within 30 working days from the reception of the request. However, there are no sanctions in case of refusal to reply or in case of a late reply.

Recommendations of advocacy reports or opinions are non-binding. However, if the recipient authority of recommendations related to state support measures or legal acts decide not to follow them, it must indicate to Pro-Competencia in writing within 30 working days which recommendations it will not comply with and the reasons for not doing so.[6] The same applies to opinions issued to sector regulators in relation to their competition enforcement actions,[7], although this is not aways happening in practice. In addition, the sector regulators with competition enforcement powers do not always consult Pro-Competencia, despite the requirement provided for in Article 20 of the Competition Act.

Since 2017, Pro-Competencia has issued 39 advocacy reports and opinions regarding different sectors (e.g. telecommunications, inland transport, food and beverages, health), as well as on other topics, such as public procurement and simplification of administrative procedures. The definition of priority areas and the follow-up of the implementation of these advocacy initiatives do not seem to be made in a consistent manner, which would benefit the overall advocacy efforts developed by Pro-Competencia.

3.1.2. Market studies

In Dominican Republic, market studies focus on the competition conditions of specific markets and propose measures to improve competition in those markets (while Pro-Competencia's reports and opinions usually target more specific rules and regulations that may have anti-competitive effects).

Items "d" and f" of Article 33 of the Competition Act grants the Pro-Competencia's Executive Directorate the power to carry out market studies to analyse the level and conditions of competition in the Dominican Republic. The Board of Directors decides together with the Executive Directorate which markets and sectors will be subject to a market study based on 10 criteria defined by the Economic and Market Studies Unit, including the classification of the market according to the Observatory of Market Conditions (see below), a preliminary evaluation of the market and the availability of information, the relevance of the selected market, the existence of barriers to entry and the impact on consumers. Market studies are developed by the Economic and Market Studies Unit.

Market studies must contain the characteristics of the markets, including the main variables determining the demand and supply, substitutes of the goods or services, main undertakings present in the supply chain and the conditions of competition, while preserving confidentiality issues and avoiding specific individualisation of market players and conducts. In addition, market studies should assess public policies and sector-specific regulation, identify barriers to entry and present the conclusions and recommendations. Market studies are made public except if Pro-Competencia has received a complaint or opened an investigation against an undertaking present in the market in question.[8]

Neither the Competition Act nor the implementing Regulation provide for a process and methodology to carry out market studies.[9] Nearly all competition authorities in OECD jurisdictions conduct some kind of market study, ranging from short and informal assessments to lengthy and formal analysis involving multiple rounds of stakeholders' input and empirical analysis. Most of them have defined a methodology and a process for carrying out market studies (OECD, 2018[3]). The OECD and the International Competition Network (ICN) have published a handbook and good practice guide on the collection and assessment of market research information (Box 3.1).

Box 3.1. The OECD-ICN Market Studies Good Practice Handbook

The OECD published a guide to market research for competition authorities in 2018. This guide should be read in conjunction with the Market Studies Good Practice Handbook prepared by the International Competition Network, which is based on the experience of the network's member authorities.

The OECD guide is structured around the main phases of market studies: the choice of market or sector, methodologies for conducting studies, including stakeholder participation, surveys, information collection and analysis, identification of market structures and their characteristics, and remedies and initiatives that could be launched as a result of such studies.

The International Competition Network Handbook provides additional detail and a wide range of useful guidance, including for:

- Planning the information gathering process, including internal consultations, determining whether the authorities already have the necessary information or can obtain it from public sources, and considering the burden on stakeholders in responding to data requests.
- Organising the research, taking into account financial constraints and considering alternatives if initial efforts prove unsuccessful. The handbook recognises that competition authorities may find it difficult to identify the most promising avenues of research at the outset of the study, and may therefore need to redirect their efforts.
- Choosing methods of information gathering, noting that empirical evidence may carry more weight than more qualitative evidence. The manual highlights the advantages and disadvantages of certain collection methods, such as targeting specific groups and surveys.
- Analysing the information, for example, whether it meets the needs of the authorities and confirms the original assumptions. Some authorities find it useful to publish initial findings and/or

possible conclusions, as this helps them to validate their findings, bring out new information, and identify possible gaps in the analysis.

- Ensuring the confidentiality of information through information handling procedures.

Source: Reproduced from OECD (OECD, 2022[4]), OECD Peer Reviews of Competition Law and Policy: Tunisia, https://www.oecd.org/daf/competition/oecd-peer-reviews-of-competition-law-and-policy-tunisia-2022.pdf.

Since 2016, Pro-Competencia has carried out 8 market studies in the following sectors and markets: (i) medicine Market (Pro-Competencia, 2016[5]); (ii) beer Market (Pro-Competencia, 2016[6]); (iii) insurance market (Pro-Competencia, 2016[7]); (iv) bread Market (Pro-Competencia, 2017[8]); (v) land transport market (Pro-Competencia, 2017[9]); (vi) management of pension funds market (Pro-Competencia, 2020[10]); (vii) public procurement and contracting processes (Pro-Competencia, 2021[11]); (viii) state support measures (Pro-Competencia, 2022[12]). At least one of them has led to a formal investigation and sanction of anti-competitive infringement by Pro-Competencia (i.e. the beer market study).

As shown in Figure 3.1 below, in 2016 the number of advocacy market studies undertaken by Pro-competencia was above the OECD average and the average number of market studies in jurisdictions with a GDP per capita similar to the Dominican Republic. However, the number of market studies published by Pro-Competencia reduced between 2017 to 2021, being below the average in the OECD, Latin America and the Caribbean, non-OECD countries and GDP per capita peers.[10] One reason for that may be the limited resources (both material and human) of Pro-Competencia and, thus, of the Economic and Market Studies Unit (see section 1.4.4).

Figure 3.1. Comparison of Number Advocacy Market Studies

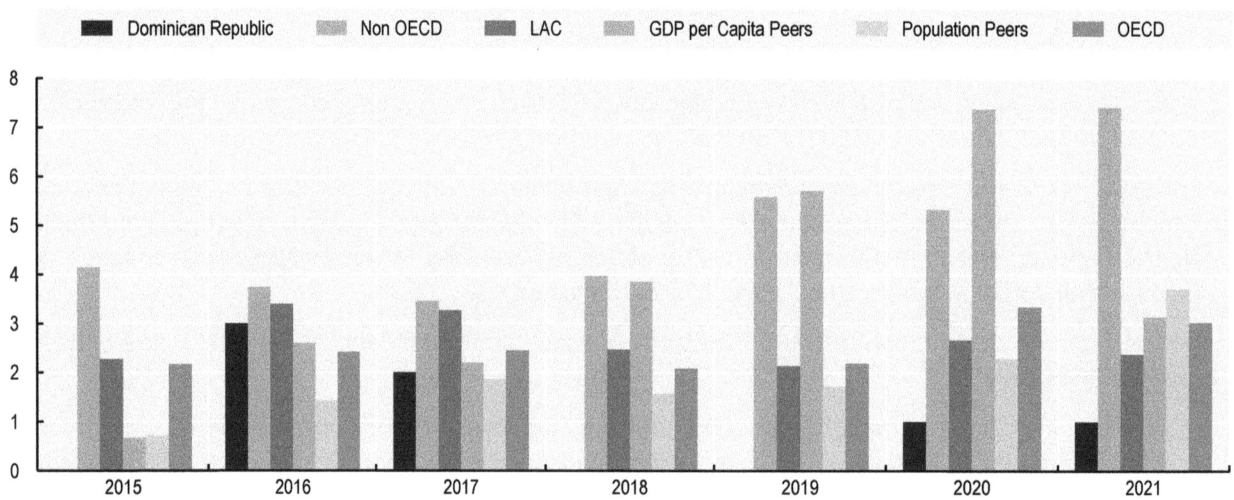

Note: OECD (2023[13]) CompStats database. https://www.oecd.org/competition/oecd-competition-trends.htm.

Box 3.2 provides an example of a market study where, in the absence of a merger control system, Pro-Competencia used its advocacy powers to analyse the competition effects of a merger in the Dominican Republic.

Box 3.2. Market Study in the beer market of the Dominican Republic, 2016

In 2016, Pro-Competencia carried out a market study to analyse the potential effects on competition of the 2012 merger between CND and AmBev, the two major breweries in the country. The transaction involved the acquisition of 51% of CND's shares by AmBev, creating a sole beverage company in the Caribbean region.

Pro-Competencia concluded that the transaction eliminated the maverick (AmBev), which since 2004 had increased the degree of competition in the Dominican beer market by lowering prices and offering a broader diversity of beer brands.

The market study also described the methodology required to define the relevant market in a competition analysis, applying the hypothetical monopolist test. Econometric methods were applied to quantify the price elasticity of demand for beer.

The market study concluded that there was a high degree of concentration in the beer market and that this had been exacerbated by the merger. It shows that, post-merger, beer prices increased, negatively affecting consumer welfare. In addition, it indicates that the horizontal integration has allowed the merged entity to increase its profit margins and its return on equity and total assets.

The market study also identified potential anti-competitive practices in the beer and the rum markets, such as exclusive dealing and tying. Part of these practices were investigated and sanctioned by Pro-Competencia in 2019 (see Box 2.3).

The market study recommended measures similar to those adopted by other competition authorities in the context of merger control procedures, including the transfer of brands; divestiture of production plants or other assets; obligation for the merged entity to grant access to its distribution network during a period of time; or prohibition of tying practices.

Source: Pro-Competencia (Pro-Competencia, 2020[14]), Study of the Competition Conditions in the Beer Market of the Dominican Republic, https://procompetencia.gob.do/wpfd_file/estudios-de-condiciones-de-competencia-en-el-mercado-de-cervezas-de-la-republica-dominicana/.

Observatory of Market Conditions

Pro-Competencia, through the Economic and Market Studies Unit, has developed the Observatory of Market Conditions (*Observatorio de condiciones de Mercado*), a tool to screen market conditions in a broad range of markets of the Dominican economy (Pro-Competencia, 2022[15]). Thanks to this tool, Pro-Competencia can better identify markets that deserve a close monitoring and, eventually, a thorough market study.

The Observatory monitors the market conditions of different sectors of the economy on the basis of 6 criteria (see Table 3.1).

Table 3.1. Criteria for the analysis of market conditions

Criteria	Definition
Criterion 1: Prices of the family market basket	Products in the family market basket that have registered atypical inflation during the period in comparison to historical trends.
Criterion 2: Economic growth	Economic sectors that have a high impact on the growth of the Gross Domestic Product (GDP) of the country.
Criterion 3: Characteristics and dynamics of the market	Market characteristics that facilitate anti-competitive behaviour, such as: high concentration and no information available on the functioning of markets generating uncertainty as to the existence of competitive pressure.
Criterion 4: Essential intermediate inputs	Economic activities that function as intermediate goods or services that are considered essential to be active in other markets.
Criterion 5: Regulations of interest	Regulatory provisions that could have an impact on conditions of competition in the markets.
Criterion 6: Societal concerns	Concerns or opinions that have been expressed by society regarding the conditions of market competition.

Source: OECD based on Pro-Competencia (Pro-Competencia, 2022[15]), Observatorio de Condiciones de Mercado, https://procompetencia.gob.do/observatorio-de-condiciones-de-mercado/.

This screening allows Pro-Competencia to identify competition risks and define priority markets either because of their structure or the behaviour of economic agents therein. Markets are then classified by colours:

a) Red includes markets that meet two or more of the evaluated criteria. It also includes markets where Pro-Competencia has opened an investigation or is about to adopt a competition infringement decision.

b) Yellow includes markets that meet one of the evaluated criteria (except for criterion 3) that also appeared in the previous screening process.

c) Green includes markets that meet one of the evaluated criteria that did not appear in the previous screening process and/or criterion 3.

This classification allows Pro-Competencia to focus its resources on monitoring markets that are more prone to competition restrictions, namely markets that have been categorised as red or orange by the Observatory.

Twice a year, Pro-Competencia publishes a report with the results of the Observatory. The report of July-December 2022 identified the following red flag markets: bread, water bread, malt, flour biscuits, sweet biscuits, health insurance services, brewing of beer, malted and malt beverage, manufacture of iron and steel products (Pro-Competencia, 2022[15]).

3.1.3. Guidelines

Issuing competition law guidelines is a common practice worldwide, aiming to spell out in advance and in a transparent fashion the competition authority's enforcement policy and approach as regards different provisions of its competition law, including both substantive and procedural aspects. Competition law guidelines usually seeks to explain the law in simpler language; indicate how a competition authority is intending to interpret the legislative provisions; refer to any relevant case law or prior decisions, which assist the competition authority with its interpretation; and provide case or hypothetical examples.

Guidelines are a powerful tool to create competition culture, particularly for developing jurisdictions where the competition culture is still emerging and where competition authorities are often young, inexperienced and faced with limited resources. Guidelines can help raise businesses and the public awareness with regard to competition law, which is likely to fosters competition compliance and competition law enforcement. Competition law guidelines may also contribute to increased legal certainty and transparency for businesses, the state, and the society. Additionally, although guidelines are not binding, they can provide guidance criteria and help establish a uniform approach in the application of competition law by the competition authority. Finally, they can help courts when analysing competition law cases, especially in jurisdictions where competition law is new.

So far, Pro-Competencia has adopted 4 public guidelines on substantive matters, while no guidelines on procedural issues have been developed. The substantive guidelines are:

a) **Guide for the prevention and detection of collusion in public procurement**: this document contains guidelines on how to prevent and detect collusive agreements in public procurement. It is a useful tool for public servants and entities involved in public procurement. It gives indications on how to design public procurement to prevent collusive practices and how to detect the most common collusive patterns (Pro-Competencia, 2020[10]).
b) **Basic guide to free competition for business and trade associations**: this guide explains the basic principles of competition enforcement in the Dominican Republic. It also provides examples of activities or initiatives of trade associations that could constitute anti-competitive conduct and gives indications on how trade associations can contribute to the prevention and fight against competition infringements (Pro-Competencia, 2020[14]).
c) **General guidelines on competition compliance programs**: this document explains the benefits and importance of having an effective competition compliance program in place. It also describes the minimum content that these programs should contain and gives a detailed explanation on how to conduct a competition risk assessment (Pro-Competencia, 2021[16]).
d) **Basic guide to the Competition Act**: this guide is aimed at providing an overview into the competition enforcement and advocacy powers of Pro-Competencia. It explains the prohibited practices, the enforcement procedures, the advocacy initiatives and the different tools available for individuals and companies willing to lodge a complaint or contact the competition authority for advocacy purposes (Pro-Competencia, 2020[14]).

In addition, at the time of writing, Pro-Competencia was updating a number of guidelines that it developed in 2015 and a frequent publication of these guidelines in Pro-Competencia's website would benefit competition advocacy and overall awareness. The topics covered include:

a) The relevant market and determination of a dominant position.
b) Concerted practices and anti-competitive agreements.
c) Abuse of a dominant position.
d) Unfair competition.
e) Reviewing State legal acts.
f) Treatment of State support measures.
g) Studies and reports on competition conditions in the markets.
h) Criteria for setting penalties.
i) Guidelines on the Competition Act for the National Congress and Public Administration entities.

3.1.4. Capacity building and outreach activities

Pro-Competencia has organised capacity-building workshops in co-operation with the United States Authority for International Development (USAID) and the Commercial Law Development Program (CLDP), providing training opportunities to officials from the competition authority and other government bodies. These workshops focused mainly on fighting bid rigging, and the General Direction for Public Procurement (*Dirección General de Compras Públicas*, DGCP) participated in most of them. These included:

a) Workshop on cartels for Pro-Competencia and DGCP staff, held during 26-28 April 2022 and 4 May 2022 by personnel from the US Department of Justice.

b) Workshop on cartel investigation techniques for Pro-Competencia and DGCP staff, held on 4 August 2022 by the staff of the CLDP and the US Department of Justice.

c) Workshops on Detecting and Deterring Collusion in Public Procurement for staff working in procurement units in different government authorities held on 10 and 11 august 2022 by personnel from the CLDP and the U.S. Department of Justice.

Pro-Competencia has also been actively participating in the OECD Regional Centre for Competition in Latin America,[11] located in Lima, which has provided several capacity-building activities in the last years that benefited 15 civil servants from Dominican Republic in 2022, 6 in 2021 and 10 in 2020.

In addition, Pro-Competencia has developed outreach events on an *ad hoc* basis, without an underlying strategy. These events focus on promoting a culture of competition to general public, such as universities, micro, small and medium-sized companies, trade associations and journalists. Table 3.2 below summarises these outreach events held by Pro-Competencia during 2018-2022. For instance, 1 018 people participated in the 22 events organised in 2022.

Table 3.2. Pro-Competencia's outreach initiatives 2018-2021

Year	Total number of outreach events organised by Pro-Competencia
2018	18
2019	10
2020	9
2021	18
2022	22

Source: Pro-Competencia.

Pro-Competencia is also very active in the media and social networks.[12] For instance, it organises regular competition-awareness campaigns through these means, which included the campaigns "*ABC competition: Sharing concepts to better understand Law 42-08*", "*Values that Compete: Sharing civil values and those of our institution to encourage fair competition*" and "*Free competition benefits us all: Campaign to promote the benefits of competition in society*".

In addition, Pro-Competencia is carrying out an essay contest for undergraduate students, aiming at promoting competition among universities (Pro-Competencia, 2023[17]). It has also recently launched an initiative called "Competition Dialogues", providing a forum for discussion on competition law issues (ProCompetencia, 2023[18]), and will publish the first Dominican Yearbook on Free and Fair Competition in October 2023.

Communication can be an effective tool to build authorities' reputation, helping to establish themselves as credible and trustworthy institutions, committed to achieving their objectives. Moreover, it educates businesses and consumers about competition law and its implications. Many businesses may not be aware of competition laws and may not fully understands their requirements. Similarly, consumers may not be able to identify anti-competitive practices. Through effective communication, authorities can help businesses and consumers understand the importance of competition and the risks of anti-competitive practices (OECD, 2023[19]).

A starting point to foster competition culture is to identify the level of awareness of competition law among business, private practitioners, public servants and citizens. This may enable the competition authority to better tailor advocacy messages and their target audience. For instance, in 2017 COFECE hired a consultancy firm to map how competition law and COFECE's actions were perceived in Mexico (McKinsey&Company, 2017[20]). This helped COFECE to adapt the language used in advocacy materials to better convey its messages to non-specialised audiences and explain in simple terms what COFECE does and how it directly benefits Mexican consumers (Mexico, 2023[21]).

3.2. Domestic co-operation

Pro-Competencia has developed co-operation channels with a number of authorities and government entities in the Dominican Republic. At national level, inter-institutional co-operation is governed by: (i) Article 138 of the Dominican Constitution, which establishes the principle of co-ordination among the entities of the Public Administration; (ii) Paragraph 4 of Article 12 of the Organic Law of Public Administration,[13] which provides for the principle of co-operation and coherent approach among the state entities; and (iii) Articles 13, 14, 20, 40 and 69 of the Competition Act.

Most of the co-operation efforts of Pro-Competencia at national level have focused on building a dialogue with sector regulators with competition enforcement powers, although there have also been some initiatives with other entities.

3.2.1. Co-ordination with sector regulators with competition enforcement powers

As previously mentioned, in the Dominican Republic, some sector regulators are given exclusive jurisdiction to enforce competition law in their respective sectors. In particular, this is the case is in the telecommunications sector, the electricity sector, the financial and banking sector, the inland transport sector, as well as for intellectual property.

In any case, co-operation between competition authorities and sector regulators are necessary to guarantee consistency between their actions, reduce duplication and ensure a more efficient and better use of public resources (OECD, 2022[22]). The Competition Act recognises the relevance of domestic co-operation and empowers Pro-Competencia and the sector regulators to adopt co-ordination initiatives. Article 69 of the Competition Act establishes that Pro-Competencia should meet with different regulators to jointly design the competition regime that would govern the different sectors and activities up to 2019. Nevertheless, this multi-lateral effort never occurred.

The creation of working groups bringing together the competition authority and a number of regulators have proven effective in other jurisdictions, improving communication and facilitating discussions between the authorities to reach a shared understanding and approach. For instance, the UK Competition Network illustrates how working groups can help enhance co-operation between the competition authority and regulators, as described in Box 3.3 (OECD, 2022[22]).

Box 3.3. UK Competition Network

The UK Competition Network is a forum for co-operation between the Competition and Markets Authority (CMA), the UK competition authority, and all sector regulators in the UK that have competition law powers within their sectors. The sector regulators that are members of the UK Competition Network are: the Civil Aviation Authority (CAA), the Financial Conduct Authority (FCA), the Gas and Electricity Markets Authority (Ofgem), the Northern Ireland Authority for Utility Regulation (NIAUR), the Office of Communications (Ofcom), the Office of Rail and Road (ORR), the Payment Systems Regulator (PSR) and the Water Services Regulation Authority (Ofwat).

The UK Competition Network aims to facilitate co-operation and to consider more generally how best to promote competition and competitive outcomes for the benefit of consumers in the regulated sectors.

For example, the Network organises workshops on procedural or substantive issues; publishes information on cases in regulated sectors; and produces an annual report dealing with competition enforcement in regulated sectors and reporting on co-operation in the previous year, such as information sharing and case allocation.

Source: OECD (2022[22]), Interactions between competition authorities and sector regulators, https://www.oecd.org/competition/interactions-between-competition-authorities-and-sector-regulators.htm; UK Government (2017[23]), UK Competition Network, https://www.gov.uk/government/groups/uk-competition-network.

In addition to the multi-lateral fora, the Competition Act sets up a consultation and a referral mechanism between Pro-Competencia and the different regulators.[14] The Competition Act requires that regulators request to Pro-Competencia an opinion regarding competition infringement decisions before its adoption. Regulators are also required to submit the draft of sector regulations to Pro-Competencia for an opinion if they involve competition law aspects. Likewise, if Pro-Competencia receives a complaint falling under the competition enforcement powers of another regulator, it must forward the complainant to the competent entity.

In order to formalise and regulate the consultation and referral procedures, Pro-Competencia and all regulators with competition enforcement powers (except for the financial and banking regulators) have signed the following bilateral co-operation agreements:[15]

Table 3.3. Co-operation agreements between Pro-Competencia and sector regulators with competition powers

Institution	Date of signature
National Office of Industrial Property (ONAPI)	02 July 2014
National Energy Commission (CNE)	01 February 2016
National Institute of Inland Transport (INTRANT)	12 September 2017
Dominican Institute of Telecommunications (INDOTEL)	06 July 2018
Superintendency of Electricity (SIE)	14 August 2018

Source: OECD based on Pro-Competencia's data.

At the time of writing, Pro-Competencia had referred a number of complaints to sector regulators, such as INTRANT, INDOTEL and SIE.[16] All cases are still ongoing or have been dismissed.

Pro-Competencia has also adopted non-binding opinions in response to the public consultations of draft sector regulations, especially regarding the inland transport sector. However, Pro-Competencia had not been consulted by any sector regulator in relation to competition enforcement decisions, which may at least partially be explained by the limited competition enforcement activity of regulators.

Several stakeholders have expressed concerns over the few competition enforcement decisions adopted by sector regulators. For instance, the competition enforcement activity of INDOTEL in the last 25 years has been modest if compared to similar sector regulators with competition enforcement powers in the region. Between 2014 and 2018, for example, the Federal Institute of Telecommunications (*Instituto Federal de Telecomunicaciones*, IFT), the regulator and competition authority for the telecommunications and broadcasting sectors in Mexico has adopted four competition infringement decisions (OECD, 2020[24]). The Superintendency of Telecommunications (*Superintendecia de Telecomunicaciones*, SUTEL), the regulator and competition authority for the telecommunications sector in Costa Rica, opened 20 investigations against anti-competitive practices between 2014 and 2018. Since 2016, SUTEL has also carried out 14 market studies into competitive conditions in various telecommunications markets (OECD, 2020[25]).

Concerns about regulatory capture[17] and how this could affect the competition enforcement activity of sector regulators has also been raised during the fact-finding mission. According to the *OECD Multi-*

Dimensional Review of Dominican Republic, policy capture is presumably high in the Dominican Republic and one of the main barriers to inclusive and sustainable development (OECD, 2022[26]).

For many years, the perception that powerful groups dominate public policy making has been extremely high in the Dominican Republic, although there has been a significant decline more recently. In fact, the perception of concentration of power has been varying between 70% and 90% since 2008, above the LAC average. In 2020, however, there was a reduction in these numbers, as around 60% of Dominican believed the country was governed for and by powerful groups, which is below the LAC average (OECD, 2022[26]).

Sometimes, policy capture can take place through private sector influence from and within the institutional framework, not from outside (OECD, 2022[26]). For example, this can occur when there is presence of private sector representatives in governing bodies of public institutions. As described in Section 1.5.1, this is the case of INDOTEL, where representatives of the regulated agents (one representing the broadcasters and another representing the telecommunications providers) seat at the Board of Directors.

3.2.2. Co-ordination with Pro-Consumidor

The Competition Act defines unfair competition as any practice contrary to good faith and business ethics in economic activities that aims at illegitimately diverting consumer demand and can be sanctioned irrespective of whether the parties involved are competitors in the market.[18] The non-exhaustive list of unfair competition practices include acts of undue comparison, acts of imitation, violation of business secrets, and acts of business defamation (e.g. thorough inexact or untrue information).[19]

Most complaints received by Pro-Competencia relate to unfair competition practices (around 50% of complaints since 2017), and internal estimations suggest that this topic covers around 80% of staff-time dedicated to investigations in Pro-Competencia. Since 2022, following a decision issued by the Board of Directors, Pro-Competencia has tried to limit the unfair competition cases to those that seriously disturb the public economic interest. Consequently, complaints affecting only private interests should be solved before civil or commercial courts.[20]

Indeed, Pro-Competencia's efforts seem in line with other jurisdictions that also have competences over unfair competition practices, given that competition authorities should focus resources on investigations that can affect the public interest, particularly the structure of market (but not those that affect private interests only).

Box 3.4. Role of competition authorities on unfair competition practices

In **Colombia**, a private party injured by unfair-competition practices may file a suit in the general or specialised commercial law courts, seeking injunctive relief and damages. The Superintendence of Industry and Commerce (*Superintendencia de Industria y Comercio*, SIC), in charge of enforcing competition law in Colombia, will only examine unfair competition claims when they harm the public interest.

In **Ecuador**, the Competition Authority (*Superintendencia de Competencia Económica,* SCE) only deals with unfair competition cases if the infringer has market power. Unfair acts that affect only individual interests are heard by civil courts, in accordance with Article 26 of Organic Law of Regulation and Control of Market Power.

In **Spain**, the Competition Authority (*Comisión Nacional de los Mercados y la Competencia*, CNMC) only investigates acts of unfair competition that affect the public interest when seriously disturbing the competitive structure or functioning of the market. Unfair-competition cases dealing with private interests are prosecuted and sanctioned by commercial judges.

Source: OECD-IDB (2021[27]), OECD-IDB Peer Reviews of Competition Law and Policy Ecuador, https://www.oecd.org/daf/competition/ecuador-oecd-idb-peer-reviews-of-competition-law-and-policy-2021.pdf; OECD (2016[28]), Colombia: Assessment of Competition Law and Policy, https://www.oecd.org/daf/competition/Colombia-assessment-competition-report-2016.pdf; Article 3 of the Spanish Competition Defence Law.

Unfair competition practices are not usually covered by competition law, being more often associated to consumer protection policies and better placed in this front. This may also explain why the line distinguishing the jurisdiction of the National Institute for the Protection of Consumer Rights (*Instituto Nacional de Protección de los Derechos del Consumidor,* Pro-Consumidor), the entity in charge of consumer protection in the Dominican Republic, and Pro-Competencia is unclear and sometimes overlap. There are no formal rules to avoid inconsistent decisions and divergent views between Pro-Consumidor and Pro-Competencia, but co-ordination efforts seem to be in place as seen by the signature of a co-operation agreement on 9 May 2017, although developments are still pending, including co-ordinated strategies, as provided for in the agreement.

3.2.3. Co-operation with other entities

As mentioned above, co-operation initiatives between the competition authority and regulators with competition powers have been more developed in the Dominican Republic, but Pro-Competencia has also been engaging with other key state entities. In this context, ten bilateral co-operation agreements were signed between Pro-Competencia and the following institutions:

Table 3.4. Bilateral co-operation agreements

Institution	Date of signature
General Directorate of Customs (*Dirección General de Aduanas*, DGA)	01 February 2017
Civil Aviation Board (*Junta de Aviación Civil*, JAC)	23 March 2018
Superintendency of the Stock Market (*Superintendencia de Mercado de Valores*, SIMV)	20 June 2018
Dominican Port Authority (*Autoridad Portuaria Dominicana*, APORDOM)	28 June 2018
Superintendence of Pensions (*Superintendencia de Pensiones*, SIPEN)	27 July 2018
General Directorate of Public Procurement (*Dirección General de Compras Públicas*, DGCP)	09 December 2020
Constitutional Court (*Tribunal Constitucional*, TC)	05 March 2022
National Institute of Civil Aviation (*Instituto Nacional de Aviación Civil*, IDAC)	10 March 2022
National Copyright Office (*Oficina Nacional de Derechos de Autor*, ONDA)	25 January 2023

Source: OECD based on Pro-Competencia's data.

However, the existence of an agreement does not ensure that co-operation will occur in practice. In fact, the level of co-operation depends to a great extent on the interest and willingness of the entities to develop concrete collaborative initiatives.

A good example of co-operation is the inter-institutional agreement signed between Pro-Competencia and the DGCP, the public procurement governing body in the Dominican Republic, to co-ordinate enforcement actions and exchange information. This agreement has set up a framework to (i) develop working groups composed of technical staff from both institutions to identify the respective roles in the prevention, detection, investigation and sanctioning of bid rigging, as well as to (ii) grant Pro-Competencia access to the Integrated Consultation System of the DGCP, allowing a faster and more direct screening of suppliers and procurement patterns. In particular, the DGCP's platform allows Pro-Competencia to obtain information regarding public procurement processes since 2017, including suppliers and the bidding procedures in which they have participated, which may be useful to detect and sanction bid rigging in public procurement in the Dominican Republic.

3.3. International co-operation

The Competition Act states that Pro-Competencia, through the Board of Directors, may sign international co-operation agreements with foreign competition authorities, as well as promote international co-operation in order to perform its activities more effectively.[21]

At the time of writing, Pro-Competencia had signed international agreements on competition issues with the following competition authorities:

Table 3.5. International co-operation agreements

Competition authority/Jurisdiction	Date of signature
National Commission for the Defense of Competition (*Comisión Nacional de Defensa de la Competencia*, CNDC), Argentina	3 February 2023
Commission for Defence and Promotion of Competition (*Comisión para la Defensa y Protección del Consumidor*, CDPC), Honduras	September 2019
Federal Economic Competition Commission (*Comisión Federal de Competencia Económica*, COFECE), Mexico	April 2016
Authority for the Protection of Consumers and Defense of Competition (Autoridad de Protección al Consumidor y Defensa de la Competencia, ACODECO) of Panama	October 2015
Market Power Control Superintendence (*Superintendencia de Control de Poder de Mercado*, SCPM), Ecuador	November 2014
National Competition Commission (*Comisión Nacional de Competencia*, CNC), Spain	September 2012*

Note: * At the time of writing, this agreement was being renegotiated with the Spanish National Commission on Markets and Competition (*Comisión Nacional de los Mercados y la Competencia*, CNMC).
Source: OECD based on Pro-Competencia's data.

These are first-generation co-operation agreements, focusing on the sharing of experiences and knowledge and on capacity-building activities. Thanks to these agreements, Pro-Competencia staff has participated in diverse exchange programmes, trainings, study visits, and internships in other countries. The agreements do not provide for deeper co-operation activities, such as sharing of confidential information, investigative assistance and joint enforcement actions with other competition authorities.

Finally, Pro-Competencia has been participating in international fora, such as the OECD Global Forum on Competition (GFC), which meets annually.[22] Pro-Competencia is also a member of the International Competition Network (ICN). At the regional level, Pro-Competencia has also actively participated in the IDB/OECD Latin American and Caribbean Competition Forum (LACCF)[23] and the workshops of the OECD Regional Centre for Competition in Latin America in Lima.

Main findings

The main findings on competition advocacy and institutional co-operation of competition law and policy in the Dominican Republic include:

- Lack of overall competition culture in the Dominican Republic.
- Insufficient levels of co-operation between Pro-Competencia and sector regulators in the application of competition law, in addition to concerns on possible conflicting interests and lack of competition expertise within certain regulatory entities with the powers to enforce competition law.
- Pro-Competencia's opinions on advocacy initiatives are non-binding. Although authorities need to justify if they decide not to follow Pro-Competencia's recommendations, this does not aways happen in practice. In addition, the sector regulators with competition enforcement powers do not always consult Pro-Competencia despite the legal requirement.
- The number of market studies conducted by Pro-Competencia is below the average for international and regional standards.

References

Dominican Republic (2022), *Subsidies, Competition and Trade - Contribution from the Dominican Republic*,, https://one.oecd.org/document/DAF/COMP/GF/WD(2022)55/en/pdf. [33]

IDB (2021), *Dominican Republic, IDB Group Country Strategy 2021-2024*. [29]

McKinsey&Company (2017), *Estudio y análisis de la percepción sobre temas de competencia económica y la labor de la COFECE - Informe de Resultados - 2017*, https://www.cofece.mx/wp-content/uploads/2018/01/Estudio-labor-COFECE-17.pdf. [20]

Mexico (2023), *Assessing and Communicating the Benefits of Competition Interventions – Note by Mexico*, https://one.oecd.org/document/DAF/COMP/WP2/WD(2023)9/en/pdf. [21]

OECD (2023), *Competition and Innovation: A Theoretical Perspective, OECD Competition Policy Roundtable Background Note*, https://www.oecd.org/daf/competition/competition-and-innovation-a-theoretical-perspective-2023.pdf. [19]

OECD (2023), *OECD Services Trade Restrictiveness Index: Policy trends up to 2023*, OECD Publishing, https://www.oecd.org/trade/topics/services-trade/. [13]

OECD (2022), *Interactions between competition authorities and sector regulators: OECD Competition Policy Roundtable Background Note*, OECD Publishing, https://www.oecd.org/competition/interactions-between-competition-authorities-and-sector-regulators.htm. [22]

OECD (2022), *Multi-dimensional Review of the Dominican Republic: Towards Greater Well-being for All, OECD Development Pathways*, OECD Publishing, https://doi.org/10.1787/23087358. [26]

OECD (2022), "OECD Peer Reviews of Competition Law and Policy: Tunisia", https://www.oecd.org/daf/competition/oecd-peer-reviews-of-competition- (accessed on 22 August 2022). [4]

OECD (2020), *Costa Rica: Assessment of Competition Law and Policy 2020, OECD Publishing*,, https://www.oecd.org/daf/competition/costa-rica-assessment-of-competition-law-and-policy2020.pdf. [25]

OECD (2020), *OECD Telecommunication and Broadcasting Review of Brazil 2020*, OECD Publishing, https://doi.org/10.1787/30ab8568-en. [24]

OECD (2019), *Executive Summary of the Roundtable on Competition issues in labour markets*, https://one.oecd.org/document/DAF/COMP/M(2019)1/ANN2/FINAL/en/pdf. [2]

OECD (2018), *Suspensory Effects of Merger Notifications and Gun Jumping, OECD Competition Policy Roundtable Background Note*, https://www.oecd.org/daf/competition/suspensory-effects-of-merger-notifications-and-gun-jumping-2018.pdf. [3]

OECD (2017), *Sustaining Iceland's fisheries through tradeable quotas, OECD Environment Policy Paper No. 9*. [31]

OECD (2016), *Local Nexus and Jurisdictional thresholds in merger control, OECD Competition Policy Roundtable Background Note*, https://one.oecd.org/document/DAF/COMP/WP3(2016)4/REV1/en/pdf. [28]

OECD (2013), *Competition Issues in Television and Broadcasting, OECD Competition Policy Roundtable Background Note*, https://www.oecd.org/daf/competition/competition-television-broadcasting.htm. [1]

OECD-IDB (2021), *OECD-IDB Peer Reviews of Competition Law and Policy Ecuador, OECD Publishing,*, https://www.oecd.org/daf/competition/ecuador-oecd-idb-peer-reviews-of-competition-law-and-policy-2021.pdf. [27]

ProCompetencia (2023), *ProCompetencia realiza el primer de varios encuentros de "Diálogos de Competencia"*, https://procompetencia.gob.do/procompetencia-realiza-el-primer-de-varios-encuentros-de-dialogo-de-competencia/. [18]

Pro-Competencia (2023), *Escribiendo por la competencia*, https://procompetencia.gob.do/escribiendo-por-la-competencia/. [17]

Pro-Competencia (2022), *El Impacto de Ayudas Estatales desde la Perspective de la Competencia: El caso de la ley 18-01 de Desarrikki Fronterizo*, https://procompetencia.gob.do/wpfd_file/estudio-sobre-el-impacto-de-las-ayudas-estatales/. [12]

Pro-Competencia (2022), *El Impacto de Ayudas Estatales desde la Perspective de la Competencia: El caso de la ley 18-01 de Desarrikki Fronterizo*, https://procompetencia.gob.do/wpfd_file/estudio-sobre-el-impacto-de-las-ayudas-estatales. [30]

Pro-Competencia (2022), *Observatorio de Condiciones de Mercado,*, https://procompetencia.gob.do/observatorio-de-condiciones-de-mercado/. [15]

Pro-Competencia (2021), *Estudio de condiciones de competencia en los procesos de compras y contrataciones públicas en la República Dominicana*, https://procompetencia.gob.do/wpfd_file/estudio-de-condiciones-de-competencia-en-los-procesos-de-compras-y-contr. [11]

Pro-Competencia (2021), *Plan de Cumplimiento*, https://procompetencia.gob.do/?s=plan+de+cumplimiento. [16]

Pro-Competencia (2020), *Estudio de Condiciones de Competencia en el Mercado de las Administradoras de Fondos de Pensiones (AFP) en la República Dominicana en el sistema de capitalización individual*, https://procompetencia.gob.do/wpfd_file/estudio-de-condi. [10]

Pro-Competencia (2020), *Estudios de Condiciones de Competencia en el Mercado de cervezas de la República Dominicana*, https://procompetencia.gob.do/wpfd_file/estudios-de-condiciones-de-competencia-en-el-mercado-de-cervezas-de-la-republica-dominicana. [14]

Pro-Competencia (2017), *Decision n. 038-2017*, https://procompetencia.gob.do/wp-content/uploads/2020/03/de-038-17-que-declara-la-incompetencia-de-atribucion-td-altice.pdf. [32]

Pro-Competencia (2017), *Estudios de Condiciones de Competencia en el Mercado del Pan de Agua y Sobao*, https://procompetencia.gob.do/wpfd_file/estudios-de-condiciones-de-competencia-en-el-mercado-del-pan-de-agua-y-sobao. [8]

Pro-Competencia (2017), *Estudios de Condiciones de Competencia en el Mercado Transporte de la República Dominicana*, https://procompetencia.gob.do/wpfd_file/estudios-de-condiciones-de-competencia-en-el-mercado-transporte-de-la-republica-dominicana/. [9]

Pro-Competencia (2016), *Estudios de Condiciones de Competencia en el Mercado de cervezas de la República Dominicana*, https://procompetencia.gob.do/wpfd_file/estudios-de-condiciones-de-competencia-en-el-mercado-de-cervezas-de-la-republica-dominicana. [6]

Pro-Competencia (2016), *Estudios de Condiciones de Competencia en el Mercado de Medicamentos*, https://procompetencia.gob.do/wpfd_file/estudios-de-condiciones-de-competencia-en-el-mercado-de-medicamentos. [5]

Pro-Competencia (2016), *Estudios de Condiciones de Competencia en el Mercado de Seguros*, https://procompetencia.gob.do/wpfd_file/estudios-de-condiciones-de-competencia-en-el-mercado-de-seguros. [7]

UK Government (2017), *UK Competition Network*, https://www.gov.uk/government/groups/uk-competition-network. [23]

Notes

[1] Articles 13, 14, 15, 20 and 31, item "n" of the Competition Act.

[2] Article 14 of the Competition Act and Article 12 of the Implementing Regulation.

[3] Article 15 of the Competition Act and Article 12 of the Implementing Regulation.

[4] Article 13 of the Competition Act and Article 11 of the Implementing Regulation.

[5] Article 20 and item "m" of Article 31 of the Competition Act.

[6] Article 13, item 2 of the Implementing Regulation.

[7] Article 16, item 7 of the Implementing Regulation.

[8] Paragraph 1 of Article 15 of the Implementing Regulation.

[9] At the time of writing, the Economic and Market Studies Unit was developing a guidance on market studies, in line with international best practices.

[10] Nevertheless, at the time of writing, Pro-Competencia was finalising a number of market studies, including in the vehicle market and the role of digital platforms, as well as in the following sectors: water bottles, cement, napkins, construction rod, vitamins, lubricants, sugar, garlic, oxygen and diapers.

[11] The OECD Regional Centre for Competition in Latin America was created in November 2019 as a joint venture between the Peruvian Competition Authority (INDECOPI) and the OECD. The Centre aims to expand the OECD's work on competition in Latin America through capacity-building and specific training to competition officials from the region. For more information, see https://www.oecd.org/daf/competition/oecd-regional-centre-for-competition-in-latin-america.htm.

[12] See, for instance, https://www.instagram.com/pcompetenciard and https://www.youtube.com/@procompetenciard.

[13] Ley Orgánica de la Administración Publica No. 247-12, https://mt.gob.do/transparencia/images/docs/marco_legal_de_transparencia/leyes/2018/Ley-247-12-Organica-Administracion-Publica2c-de-fecha-9-de-agosto-de-2012.pdf.

[14] Article 20 of the Competition Act.

[15] However, it should be noted that Pro-Competencia and the Superintendency of Banks have been strengthening their relationship, in order to foster competition in the financial and banking sector (IDB, 2021[29]).

[16] For instance, on 5 December 2017, Pro-Competencia forwarded to INTRANT a complaint received from the Union of Drivers and Employees of Minibuses (*Sindicato de Choferes y Empleados de Microbuses*, SICHOEM), for alleged anti-competitive practices (Pro-Competencia, 2017[9]). On 26 October 2017, Pro-Competencia adopted a decision stating that it did not have the powers to investigate a complaint from TRILOGY DOMINICANA, S.A. against ALTICE HISPANIOLA, S.A. and TRICOM, S.A. for alleged unfair competition practices in the market for the provision of telecommunications services, and the case was forwarded to INDOTEL (Pro-Competencia, 2017[32]). On 21 September 2022, Pro-Competencia forwarded to SIE a complaint received from the Dominican Alliance against Corruption (*Alianza Dominicana Contra la Corrupción*, ADOCCO) regarding the alleged participation of an electricity company (Norther Electricity Distribution Company, EDENORTE) in a bid-rigging scheme (Pro-Competencia, 2022[15]).

[17] Policy capture is "*the process of consistently or repeatedly directing public policy decisions away from the public interest towards the interests of a specific interest group or person*" (OECD, 2017[31]).

[18] Article 10 of the Competition Act.

[19] Article 11 of the Competition Act.

[20] Decision No. 009-2022 from 15 November 2022 (Pro-Competencia, 2022[30]). This Decision has been contested by different stakeholders. The main argument is that Pro-Competencia is required by law to investigate all complaints that it receives (Article 36 of the Competition Act) and would not be empowered to adopt decisions limiting its enforcement obligations.

[21] Items "s" and "t" of Article 31 of the Competition Act.

[22] For instance, in 2022 Pro-Competencia has submitted a written contribution to the Roundtable on Subsidies, Competition and Trade (Dominican Republic, 2022[33]).

[23] In 2012, Pro-Competencia hosted the 10th meeting of the LAACF.

4. Recommendations

This section will present recommendations, related to the institutional and legal framework, competition law enforcement, as well as competition advocacy and institutional co-operation. They suggest possible ways forward for consideration by the Dominican Republic, with the aim of improving the country's competition law and policy. For a list of the key recommendations which seem particularly relevant for the improvement of competition law and policy in the Dominican Republic, see the Executive Summary of this report.

4.1. Institutional and legal framework

- Adopt a common competition framework, including both substantive and procedural rules, that uniformly applies across all sectors. In addition, clarify which entities are responsible for the enforcement of competition law in the different sectors (i.e. Pro-Competencia or sector regulators).
- Strengthen budgetary and human resources dedicated to competition enforcement in Dominican Republic:
  - Increase Pro-Competencia's budget (e.g. through governmental funding, administrative fees of a future merger control regime, and resources from international co-operation agreements, and avoid the use of sanctions for this purpose).
  - Provide Pro-Competencia with more staff dedicated to core competition functions (e.g. hiring staff, transferring civil servants from other entities, converting current administrative positions into positions allocated to competition functions).
  - Review the remuneration of technical staff to make Pro-Competencia more attractive as a long-term employer, as well as introduce credible career plans for temporary employees.

  - Provide Pro-Competencia with the necessary resources to invest in a digital case management system, IT forensics and computers able to run sophisticated software for data analytics.
  - Offer trainings to Pro-Competencia's staff on competition and economics.
- Enable Pro-Competencia to prioritise enforcement and advocacy actions based on transparent criteria (e.g. economic and geographic impact, relevance to consumers, public procurements or strategic industries), including the power not to take enforcement actions or to close investigations based on its priorities and/or availability of resources.
- Adopt the necessary institutional safeguards to guarantee the independence of the competition enforcement actions of Pro-Competencia and sector regulators with competition enforcement powers as per OECD Recommendation on Transparency and Procedural Fairness in Competition Law Enforcement.

4.2. Merger control

- Adopt a general ex-ante merger control regime in line with OECD standards and international best practices, in particular:
  - The delineation of merger control jurisdiction through the definition of mergers, the selection a merger notification mechanism and the determination of notification thresholds;
  - The establishment of a transparent, effective and timely merger review procedure, and corresponding merger review powers with Pro-Competencia;
  - The provision of a consistent substantive test to assess mergers' impact on competition;
  - The enforceability of merger control rules through adequate enforcement tools, sanctions and judicial review.
- While a general merger control regime is not implemented in the Dominican Republic, ensure that the existing merger control regime in the telecommunications, electricity and financial sectors take into account the effects on competition of the transactions and that Pro-Competencia is consulted in all reviews.

4.3. Anti-competitive practices

- Increase enforcement actions against cartels and abuse of dominance cases:
  - Detection, standard of proof and scope of infringements
    - Develop effective anti-cartel detection tools such as pro-active methods (e.g. economic filters and industry monitoring) and anonymous complaints.
    - Ensure that hard core cartels are considered *per se* infringements.
    - Monitor anti-competitive vertical agreements and ensure that they are covered by the legislation and the enforcement practice.
    - Adopt a broader concept of restriction on competition when assessing anti-competitive behaviours, not limited to unjustified market barriers.
  - Sanctions, settlements and leniency
    - Ensure that sanctions have sufficient deterrent effects. Maximum caps of fines should be based on flexible elements that allow to consider the specific circumstances of the cases and the markets affected in line with international standards (e.g. percentage of turnover).
    - Introduce non-monetary sanctions for anti-competitive infringements, such as director disqualification and bidder exclusion.

    - Ensure that individuals who have participated in anti-competitive practices are administratively sanctioned.
    - Ensure that the current criminal law provision is effectively enforced against cartels.
    - Adopt general guidelines on the methodology to impose sanctions and calculate fines, considering not only the damage caused by the anti-competitive practice but other elements such as length and severity of infringement.
    - Improve the existing settlement mechanisms (i.e. Pro-Competencia's Decisions Nº. 008-2011 and Nº. 011-2021), particularly in parallel with more enforcement decisions and higher sanctions.
    - Introduce a proper leniency policy to be implemented when the enforcement activities of Pro-Competencia are more effective, including with deterrent sanctions.
  - Interim measures
    - Clarify that Pro-Competencia can adopt interim measures to effectively cease possible infringements, subject to judicial review.
- Improve the procedural framework for enforcement actions:
  - Timeline of investigations
    - Expand the length of the statute of limitation in line with international practices.
    - Increase the timeline limitation to conduct investigations and/or allow for more flexibility regarding the extension or suspension of investigation deadlines.
  - Dawn raids
    - Ensure that dawn raids can be conducted before notifying the alleged offending parties of the initiation of a formal investigation, in order to ensure the surprise effect.
    - Streamline the procedure for requesting authorisations for dawn raids, ensuring that they can be directly requested by Pro-Competencia's Executive Directorate solely based on indications of anti-competitive infringements.
  - Transparency and procedural fairness
    - Protect the investigation phase, for instance by allowing Pro-Competencia to publish non-confidential versions of the decision to initiate the investigation and the complaints (instead of the full version) after the opening of the formal investigations.
    - Ensure that confidential information other than business secrets is protected during and after investigations. In addition, clarify the circumstances in which certain information can be disclosed.
    - Ensure that privileged communications between attorneys and clients are protected during and after investigations, for instance by setting clear guidelines on which type of client-attorney information can be considered privileged, as per OECD Recommendation on Transparency and Procedural Fairness in Competition Law Enforcement.
  - Sanctions for effective investigations
    - Establish clear and effective sanctions for companies and individuals who do not co-operate with Pro-Competencia during inspections.
    - Introduce deterrent fines for failure to reply, late replies and the use of incomplete or misleading information regarding requests of information by Pro-Competencia.

4.4. Judicial review and private enforcement

- Invest in competition-specific trainings for judges involved in competition cases, for instance with the help of international organisations.
- Consider encouraging private enforcement to allow the compensation of victims and boost the deterrent effect of competition law.

4.5. Competition advocacy

- Further promote competition within the Dominican Republic, in order to create a competition culture among businesses, government and general public. This should include a national competition advocacy strategy, with coordinated planning, priority setting, and active involvement of the relevant stakeholders.
- Further promote competition capacity-building initiatives to civil servants in charge of competition enforcement, including through resources available internationally (e.g. OECD, foreign competition authorities, ICN training on demand).
- Establish a structured follow-up of the implementation of recommendations made by Pro-Competencia's advocacy actions (e.g. reports, opinions and market studies) in order to allow the assessment of their impact and to take further actions if necessary.
- Adopt a clear methodology and process for carrying out market studies.
- Continue developing guidelines on substantive matters and adopt guidelines on procedural issues.

4.6. Domestic and International co-operation

- Ensure that co-ordination mechanisms between Pro-Competencia and the sector regulators with competition enforcement powers are effectively implemented, including the use the consultation mechanism provided for in the Competition Act regarding the adoption of competition infringement decisions and draft sector regulation. Proper channels of information sharing, staff exchanges and joint working groups should also be implemented. In addition, ensure the existence of formal co-operation agreements between Pro-Competencia and all sector regulators with competition enforcement powers.
- Ensure that government entities, including sector regulators with competition enforcement powers, explain the reasons when choosing not to follow Pro-Competencia's non-binding opinions and recommendations.
- Empower another entity (for instance, Pro-Consumidor) with the enforcement of unfair competition practices. Alternatively, Pro-Competencia should limit its investigations related to unfair competition practices to those affecting the general public economic interest, freeing up resources to competition infringement investigations. In this case, co-operation with Pro-Consumidor, particularly in relation to unfair competition practices, should be strengthened.
- Continue developing co-operation with public procurement entities to enhance the fight against bid rigging.
- Continue developing technical co-operation with foreign competition authorities and enhance participation and engagement in international events. In addition, strengthen international co-operation efforts, such as through the sharing of confidential information, investigative assistance and joint enforcement actions with other competition authorities.

www.ingramcontent.com/pod-product-compliance
Ingram Content Group UK Ltd.
Pitfield, Milton Keynes, MK11 3LW, UK
UKHW051507290926
15471UKWH00008B/1477

9 789264 612921